"One mightier than I is coming . . . He will baptize you in the Holy Spirit and fire."

John the Baptist
(Luke 3:16)

Jesus Fields Publishing

ISBN 978-0-9957941-6-0

Printed in Great Britain by Bell and Bain Ltd, Glasgow

DEDICATION

To my beloved wife and son

ACKNOWLEDGMENTS

I would like to thank my parents John and Caroline for having me, bringing me up and loving and encouraging me until this very day. I would like to thank my beloved wife Thea for being my loudest champion and deepest support. I would like to thank Gary Oates and Bill Johnson for being spiritual fathers. I would like to thank Harriet Compston and Julia Maxfield for their editorial help and Caleb Simmons for designing the book cover. I would like to thank those brothers and sisters out there who have taken up the whole armour of God alongside me and fought the good fight, helping me to get up again and again and again. Finally, I thank the Lord Jesus for saving my life from the pit and setting me on the path of life.

FOREWORD

I first met Dom 11 years ago in 2007 on a mission trip to Brazil. I was impressed by his style of worship and his love for the Lord.

Later that year he joined our mentoring program. And to be honest, he was difficult to deal with. He was always questioning everything we were doing. It drove me crazy.

About two weeks before he was to go back to England, while praying and fasting, he had a major encounter with God. What happened? He gave up on the ministry, his girlfriend, everything! Total surrender!

I saw him make the transition from not relying upon himself, upon his own intellect, upon all self-effort, in order to follow the Lord fully – no matter what. God then restored his ministry, the same girlfriend is now his wife – everything changed. They are now the proud parents of a wonderful son!

I have the highest respect for Dom. I've often referred to him as a modern day John Wesley. His burning passion for the lost and his boldness has caused a Godly jealousy to rise up within me.

Dom is a straight shooter. He tells it like it is. He has a refreshing "out of the box" approach.

This is not just another book. It can be a source of life to those who embrace its message.

If you are serious about following the Lord, and are willing to apply the principles in this book, I promise you – your life will never be the same.

Gary Oates
Author, *Open My Eyes, Lord*

WHAT PEOPLE ARE SAYING ...

"*Fire Brand* is accurately titled, as this book is a journey into the fiery belly of the gospel. With passion and single-eyed focus, Dominic Muir takes us on a daily encounter with the power and the privilege of living for Christ. Each day's reading will inspire you to live out the reality of being sons and daughters of the Living God."

Bill Johnson, Bethel Church, Redding, CA
Author of The Way of Life and God is Good

"It is time for preachers, ministers and ordinary church goers to be on fire for Jesus. This book will light a fire in your heart to know Jesus deeper and empower you to spread the Gospel fearlessly. Firebrand is a book that is truly needed in this generation."

Daniel Chand, Walking Like Jesus Ministries

"I am grateful to know Dominic Muir. He is a living example of one who unashamedly lives out his faith in Jesus with boldness and without compromise. This book shakes me out of my complacency and leaves me challenged and stirred. It is a testament to God's glorious grace, full of depth and richness, each page will lead you deeper in your walk with Jesus. Dominic is one of God's great agitators, and if this book provokes, inspires, and reignites you, then it has done its job. Fire Brand is an appropriate title for this book, and much needed for the Church at this time. This book will spur you on."

Mark Marx, Healing on the Streets
Author, Stepping into the Impossible

"Having met Dominic while on crusade in Ethiopia I was struck by one thing in particular; I thought, here is a man who is every bit as passionate when preaching to a beggar in the gutter as he is when stood microphone in hand addressing a crowd of 10,000. Integrity, it's in short supply these days, yet Dominic lives it, and this is the strength of his book. He takes you on a journey, following the pattern of a life lived aflame. Dominic's candour and verve make *Fire Brand* a real joy to read, I recommend this wholeheartedly to all willing to answer the call of radical obedience to Christ."

Graham Phillips, Lead Pastor,
LifeSpring Church, Wolverhampton

"Dominic is a deep thinker and eloquent communicator whose passionate love for Jesus and the Gospel provokes each reader to be set ablaze with fresh hunger. You will be stirred to go deeper in your knowledge and understanding of God with this daily devotional. God is calling us into an un-compromised commitment to his life of fire and Dom's writings articulate a sober yet beautiful invitation into that place."

Tiffany Buhler, David's Tent Director

"Incredible book! I was stirred and provoked as I read this. *Fire Brand* is a beautiful reflection on the essence of Christianity, a courageous and gut-honest account of day to day living with Jesus. The style is accessible but not patronising, provocative but not manipulative. Dominic is a much-needed voice and this book is a rallying cry to believers to truly live lives worthy of their high calling."

Lucy Grimble, musician and Worship Leader

"*Fire Brand* leads you on a journey along the narrow path of devotion through the different seasons of life, embracing both the clear call and the seeming paradoxes of a life lived in surrender to Jesus. Touching on themes such as grace, wilderness, rest, identity, sacrifice, courage and zeal, this book is a wonderful resource for keeping your fires of devotion stoked. In Dom's own words, "This generation doesn't want Ted Talk sheen, clever lighting displays and bottom-kissing relevance. They long to comprehend reverence. They want something worthy of giving their lives for." A hearty Amen to that!"

Pete Portal, Tree of Life Manenberg
Author of No Neutral Ground

"Fire is caught; not taught. It takes more than a detailed definition of devotion to ignite a man or woman for God. It takes words that bleed out from life broken open in private worship. The words in this book are such words. Dominic has not just written this from a study desk – so as to reach a head. But he has written from the place where knees touch the floor – and so it reaches the heart. I commend this book of daily readings to all who are looking for strong fuel in their pursuit if the Holy One."

Joshua Jones, Pastor at Therfield Chapel
Author of Elijah Men Eat Meat

"This book is bold, brilliant and true. Be ready to be motivated, set on fire and to encounter God as you turn these pages."

Dr Francois Engelbrecht, Powerhouse Ministries, Cape Town

"Fire brands do two things: ignite other fires and tattoo hearths where they have once burned. Jesus Christ is the Great Inextinguishable, the ultimate *Fire Brand* who both ignites and sets hearts ablaze forever. Dominic Muir provokes and navigates us through the searing heat of Yahweh and His command to 'fan into flame' the precious Gift of the Holy Spirit."

Nick Franks, Firebrand Notes

"We have seen Dominic preach on the streets, in shopping malls, at times on top of post boxes and even on the roof tops of shanty towns. His passion to preach the gospel in its original undiluted form with the cross at the centre is an ongoing relentless journey that I have had the privilege and honour to witness time after time. *Fire Brand* is the fuel behind the fire Dominic carries both for the Lord and the lost souls he is chasing day and night. It's a beautiful culmination of devotionals much of which he has discovered and digested in the secret place alone with God and continues to do so. *Fire Brand* is not 'another book' that one reads and puts away on a shelf somewhere. It's a lifestyle. It's a reflection of how we are meant to live for Jesus and His unaltered message whichever circle or sphere of influence we work in. Read it. Ponder. Digest it. Then watch how the fire on the pages propel you to do the impossible."

Rahil Patel, former Hindu Priest
Author of Found By Love

"Dominic Muir is a man after God's heart. Over seventeen years of friendship, he has been a constant source of support, challenge and inspiration. He doesn't just talk the talk, he walks it too, seeking to take others with him. He is passionate, kind, bold and faithful, an artist, theologian and poet. These daily reflections embody those qualities. They will be a blessing to all who read them."

Rev Pat Allerton, Vicar, St Peter's Notting Hill

"Such power and depth — truly a book for the season giving in depth keys and revelation of what we need to be able to rise up as sons of God in this season and time. The contents of the book are so vast bringing us back to our position as sons in a place of authority and rulership. The author releases keys, facts, characteristics and principles that are Biblical and true. This devotional will take you on a journey where you will be restored back into your true identity in Christ and will truly take possession of your inheritance.

In the modern era so many authors have moved away from Jesus as the Centre point and focused on encounters. Dominic makes Jesus the Centre point again and restores you into the fullness and power of a son of God. You will be changed and transformed by reading and working through this book. *Fire Brand* is a must read and full of the true Kingdom lifestyle. In reading this book you will also realize that the author is passionate about Jesus and what he releases is not just out of knowledge, but also out of his own life encounters and testimonies. This is a brilliant book for all who desires to walk in the fullness of God in victory."

Dr. Etienne Blom, Kingdom Fire Ministries

"'Fire Brand' truly is an insight into what a life of fire looks like. Dominic thoughtfully yet boldly unpacks some of the ingredients for living all out for, and in love with Jesus - including becoming fully aware of the goodness of the Gospel, stepping into our true identity and having a right Godly mindset, as well as embracing the fullness of hope, grace, forgiveness, thankfulness, joy and truth. But at the centre of this book is a brave challenge to the Church to step up to the central calling of the gospel - to 'man up', be bold, embrace tough love, and preach the gospel. This book does what the gospel should do to our hearts - remind us we are entirely loved whilst on the wildest adventure and battle of our lives. It will stir you for the more and excite you to take up your cross and live a life worthy of the call to follow Him.

Dom is a dear friend who has had a huge impact on my life. I have watched him walk out and live this message. At a critical time for the Church in the west, I am so glad he has boldly put to paper such encouragement for us all!"

JJ Waters, Burn 24/7 UK Director

CONTENTS

My Story

Devotions from a Life of Burning

MY STORY

CHAPTER 1
"WHAT'S YOUR DRUG?"

The cowlick years

I had a happy childhood. When I remember my early years I think of birthday parties and presents under the Christmas tree and fighting with my brothers for the last chocolate biscuit in the pack. I had a dreamy time, I often got what I wanted, without wanting much, and really the only time I was unhappy was when I couldn't do a simultaneous equation or pluck up enough courage to tell a girl I fancied her.

I have two brothers and a sister and Mum and Dad would take us to church most Sundays. At the time, my Dad would have called himself Catholic and my Mother an Anglican so we would hop between the denominations and therefore never really became affiliated with one church. Going to church was never about the people, it seemed to be about the ceremony. The churches we went to were very traditional and pretty stuffy. I had a vague appreciation that a man called Jesus had claimed to be the Son of God and that He had died on a cross for our sins but I didn't see why we had to go and stand in an echoey and cold museum to recognize that.

I didn't really see the connection between Jesus and God; Jesus was a man with long hair, a beard and a slightly silly name who died hundreds of years ago. I knew that God had made the world and that we could therefore pray to Him (I don't know how I made that connection) but I didn't get the formal bit, the need for church. It was boring, inconvenient and routine and only ever happened on a Sunday before lunch when I was uncommonly hungry.

I used to pray at night by myself that Dad would get home safely from business trips abroad and that I wouldn't fail my exams at school. If my heart was involved at all, that was it. God was there but church wasn't. Or church was there and God wasn't.

When I went to boarding school at fourteen I wanted to be confirmed a Catholic because it was slightly different. I felt it would give me an edge, a sort of mystery and depth. To me Catholicism smacked of holiness and naughtiness at the same time and I liked the image that I felt it was fostering for me. If I'm honest my attitude to God was that He was most probably out there somewhere but I certainly didn't have any form of relationship with Him or sense that He loved me and had my best interests at heart.

I suppose I was getting a little older, feeling a little more worldly and learning about other things. I was wide-eyed at the rich tapestry of opportunity that lay before me. I liked the idea now that I could be a mysterious Catholic intellectual, not confined to one God necessarily, one creation story and one way of life. I wanted experience – I wanted to expand my mind. I wanted fun. Boarding school provided the perfect arena.

My first day at Eton College, aged 14.

Looking at this photo I'm pierced by a fragility and innocence that the years and the pastures of life since then have both ravaged and redeemed. I had a wonderful time at this famous establishment, in many ways – the quality of academic insight, the resources, facilities, the opportunities to act, play a plethora of sports, debate, lead, dream. I made great friendships, forged in the cauldron of shared excitement, hopes, fears and insecurities.

I was good at sport, I could paint, I was academically gifted to some extent, and I had older siblings who had tutored me in teenage survival, so this gave me some confidence. I had loving parents, cheering me on from the sidelines. But I didn't realise that I was entering a world not of abundant life but necessary survival – a world that was looking to destroy my true identity and replace it with a convincing counterfeit.

Comparison, competition, bullying, name-calling, performance and posturing were rife, thick, palpable in this culture of (spiritual) orphans in their quest to survive and justify their existence. Suddenly, was I cool enough? Was I funny enough? Was I talented enough, masculine enough? Dominic – defend yourself, fight, survive, hide, pretend. I was in a sea of fight or flight, without knowing it.

I was stripped naked by older boys on several occasions and laughed at and mocked mercilessly. These were terrifying, humiliating experiences the stinking fruit of which was decade-long agreements (mainly subconscious) with shame and rejection. Suddenly, I was a victim and didn't measure up and hyper vigilance, mask-wearing and performance would need to help me survive.

Pre-pubescent, I didn't measure up as a man under the spotlight of boarding school exposure and sexual abuse. My penis wasn't large enough, my voice not deep enough, my jaw not square enough for the false masculine "accuser", who stalked the corridors of our house like a roaring lion looking to devour innocence, purity and freedom with his lies. My chest was smooth and bony, my stash of pornography non-existent. I was naked and ashamed and I needed fig leaves of covering, fast (Genesis 2-3). Shame, fear and control had to make me a castle, a system of living, a plethora of deadly attitudes and strongholds, so that I could be safe. What I desperately needed was the intimacy of our heavenly Father, the Tree of Life, the truth of how God sees me. But despite daily chapel services (stuffy though they were), I chose independence, the fruit which kills, and slowly hid myself from God and everyone else.

So amidst the rat race of validation and in my God-given craving for belonging, acceptance and peace I sought out ways of escape, self-soothing and peer-group celebrity. At Eton there was a group of us into Trance, Indie and Brit Pop and for those of us who valued their so-called integrity this came with a side order of drugs and clubbing. We would experiment with class As, discuss religion, ethics and world views, all the while secretly desperate to 'get laid'.

Hormones and amphetamines

So at 16 I was taking acid, ecstasy, cocaine, speed, dope and drinking like a lord. It was exciting in a kind of, 'aren't I against the grain?' 'naughty but holy' kind of way. I would bomb up to London on the train and get high.

Suddenly this mind alteration freed me to explore, it seemed, the possibility that God didn't exist and that He was just something I had been taught, just as I had been taught not to take drugs. I was taught not to take drugs because they were bad for me and now I realised they were fun and when taken sensibly simply not dangerous. How much else had I been taught that was barricading my life from fun and that was apparently not true?

Drugs were fun and interesting and most importantly a crucial part of a sort of 'enlightenment' rites of passage that I certainly didn't want to be left out of. They were more real than this far off God whom people claimed lurked in and around dusty altars. Anyway, by this stage it seemed that even more people couldn't agree on who God is or was. Not only did Christians disagree but what about all these Muslims, Buddhists and Hindus? Not to mention the millions of other religions I just kept hearing about. It had to be all man made and impossible to know for sure, therefore clearly not worth worrying about. And anyway science had disproved God years ago. Or at least that is what my GCSE Biology book suggested.

In my apparent intellectual freedom I suddenly felt as though I needed to free myself from the man made crutch that professed a Creator. Then the possibilities would be endless and intriguing. Oooohhh, I remember thinking that suddenly I had walked into a tremendously exciting and alternative moral and ethical philosophy. Was there a right and a wrong? Who knew anymore? That didn't matter either, because I was fast becoming my own boss.

'Being my own boss' served up some hard lessons. In the year before my A-levels I had a terrible experience on LSD. A whole bunch of us had gathered for a party at a friend of mine's parents' country house. There would be no girls, little alcohol and the menu seemed to consist of hard drugs, coloured light bulbs and tie-dyed drapes. Even as someone who took drugs recreationally I remember thinking that this seemed a little excessive and tunnel-visioned. Everyone was on different drugs and my selection of a blue microdot (particularly strong LSD) proved disastrous.

Having come up extremely quickly with orgasmic rushes I was fast transported into another consciousness. I lost all rationale, developed terrifying paranoia, and was unable to look at anything without hallucinating. For eight hours I was deprived of all the things that provide stability: relationship, love and the concept of space and time. Instead I was met with demon spirits and what seemed like accusation and fear from the friends I most loved and a genuine belief that it would never end. It was an unspeakably frightening experience, I was tasting hell.

Maybe those guys who came to school to preach about the dangers of drugs had a point. Maybe they were doing a little more than appeasing the authorities' so-called narrow mindedness. Indeed the lessons continued to come. I suffered from terrible paranoia from this one experience for at least six months and this was further exacerbated by a good friend in my year being taken from school suddenly one afternoon and admitted to a mental hospital. We were playing cards and his voice started going funny and making high-pitched squeaks and this terrible fear came over him. Excess marijuana had brought on an apparent predisposition to schizophrenia and that was the last I saw of my friend for many years.

Temporarily chastened, I picked myself up, stiffened my upper lip and got on with it. The following year I was made a school prefect and head of house. I was also in all the teams and everything I touched seemed to turn to gold. I ruled, and people (13-year-old boys with Lamborghini posters on their walls) started to worship me and follow what I did. I had power, just so much power! I started to imagine how this power might develop throughout university and into my career. Surely it was all about me and what decisions I made – my destiny was in my own hands. Just go out and get it Dominic, I thought.

Happy clappers

I went to Newcastle University having under performed, at least I felt, in my A-levels (no offence to the great university or its talented alumni). The wind had slightly come out of my sails and I had spent the year previously developing my interest in art whilst doing some travelling. I lost my virginity in Sarasota, Florida to a girl whose name and face I can barely remember. But at least it was over and I could speak qualitatively, if not that quantitatively, about what was such an important issue to my friends and I.

I hadn't stepped foot inside a church for at least a year and my Northern student life was a cocktail of cheap lager, unappreciated lectures and pulling women in order to 'get as far as I could' with them. I no longer trusted any girl that liked me, largely owing to having had my heart broken a year previously. I thought 'I'll have sexual conquest, some mind alteration drugs and four lectures a week please.'

Apparently, certain previous lessons had already worn off. I was a hedonist and deep down I was ashamed and needed to find my identity, peace and place with my peers through partying and the "false masculine" success-sterotype which public school and the world had carefully discipled me in. Looking back, there is a fine line between fun and escape, joy and dissipation.

In my first year I was an inmate of 'Castle Leazes Halls of Residence'. I had my own little room that neighbored the head of the Christian Union. I forget his name but I remember he absolutely epitomized what I had come to see as this new and slightly pathetic brand of Christian that actually prayed in groups on a week day, had 'fellowship' (an unacceptably repulsive word) and, wait for it, 'loved Jesus'.

How could any self respecting male of the species, love the bearded tunic wearer? I'll tell you how: get a dodgy haircut, an ill-fitting sweater from 'The Sweater Shop' and smile when there's nothing to smile about. It was, he was, inconceivable to me. In fact, often we would pass each other in the corridors in our dressing gowns, clutching our tasteless wash bags and I would treat him a little like an escapee from a zoo. I would be curious, slightly unnerved and careful not to pick up too much of his scent.

University life, as I led it, began to wear. In my search for something to satisfy I bumped into more smiley Christians and sucked them into my slightly empty world only to spit them and their copious books on God out like boiled sweets that lose their appeal. Their keenness to share their faith was not only patronizing but made me feel nauseous.

Fuelled by an increasing fear of the job market and the importance of my success within it (these fig leaves of achievement would surely cover my shame?), my third year became all about 'milk round' applications and the Robinson Library. I did internship after internship and for the first time in my life put in some hard hours at the books. I was awarded a First Class degree and was finally back in the driving seat. Yes, I was now ready for the big wide world and it would have to get ready for me. I saw money, prestige and power just waiting to be seized!

CHAPTER 2
"WHAT'S YOUR IDENTITY?"

From "How do you do?" to "What do you do?"

My graduation arrived at the peak of the internet bubble, in the summer of 1999, and so, like red rag to a bull, I joined the first IT company that promised an imminent IPO with healthy share options. I saw myself being catapulted, eighties style, into wealth and glamour. A sort of executive, corporate, business card and conference suite glamour – if such a thing ever existed.

My life fast became about sharp suits and night club guest lists. I was never mad keen on the business side of things but longed to present in front of the board, about what it didn't matter, before tearing off to a night-club to demolish five double vodka red bulls. And that's exactly what I did! The internet industry at that time was spiraling out of control and adolescent funsters like myself, who only weeks previously had learned to send an e-mail, were suddenly revered in the media world simply because they were still likely to grow out of their new black Gucci loafers.

My spirituality was at an all-time low: I now saw church as an opiate for the people and not nearly as good as the real thing. Staring at a screen in a corporate environment was never really me though. I suppose websites, the end product, easily failed to justify the means. Soon it didn't matter how much my salary was raised and what my business card said – I was just bored. I spent more and more of my work time surfing the net for purposes that were simply not work-related and began to develop an interest in internet pornography.

Like most addictions that won't stand still I wanted more and quite soon I was immersed in chat rooms, internet dating and then internet swinging. It was the most exciting thing I had ever been involved in, but it was that dark excitement, far from the innocent, childlike excitement that seemed more and more out of reach. It was all behind closed doors and arrangements and meetings were risky and illicit.

My office and social life became an intoxicating combination of 'Eyes Wide Shut' and 'Wall Street' (for the film buffs out there) or at least that was my goal. It felt strangely glamorous and I was quite impressed with myself. I was lost and beginning to slip, in many ways actually, but the only way that mattered to me at the time, was in terms of my career.

So I left what in retrospect was really a grasping for power and money, appeased by a 'white collar' respectability and mildly creative bent, and turned my hand to the film industry – the mouth-watering prospect of 'true creativity', glamour and fame. Now, I must stress at this stage that my motivations for entering these industries were my motivations. You readers involved in these industries may not have the same motivations. So forgive me if I'm apparently offending your vocation and your integrity! I'm not – intentionally, anyway. But if you're motivations are idolatrous then I make no apology for rattling your cage!

I can only try to be honest with what I perceive were at the root of some of my actions. I had always had a creative instinct so I genuinely thought that this might catch fire at a film course at NYU (New York University). If it didn't then there was always the hotbed of Manhattan to fall back on. Indeed my time as an Englishman in New York was alien to the nightlife I had grown up in. It was electric and it never ended. I was sky high on the buzz of the Big Apple for four months and returned to London champing at the bit for a job in Soho.

I did however pick up some terrible habits in New York. Gripped by financial dire straits I would steal sandwiches from the university union canteen. For some reason, I easily justified this occasional 'liberty' upon quick reflection of the astronomic university fees and the fact that this poor, hard working student was also having to work four nights a week as a waiter. I sometimes wonder if there might have been something lurking in the thrill of getting away with this petty theft. I'm not convinced though.

I had started to make short films in my spare time, was watching foreign films avidly for homework and really thought that my ship had finally come in. I just sensed for the first time that I had found a career that matched my passion. Following several weeks of aggressive and imaginative job applications (even if I do say so myself), with a typical slice of nepotism, I landed a job in one of the best film production companies in London.

I was employed as a 'runner', and would relish delivering cups of tea to revered film directors. These guys were so cool that I quickly realised I was moving and shaking with a different species of human. On my first day of work I was offered a line of cocaine off the board room table by the managing director, which I duly accepted, conscious to pass any initiation test with flying colours. Soon I realised that my wardrobe would need to have a serious makeover and then finally my 't's' would have to go if my accent were not to betray any inherent talent or creativity that I might have lurking behind my privileged, ex public school exterior.

I worked amazingly hard in my bid for fast promotion. And it worked. Within six months I was pulling together film crews and was on first name terms with award winning film directors. I was partying with them and worshipping them, snorting and drinking at the altar, inadvertently chasing after that heady mix of inebriation and fear.

I remember vividly the moment when the film world came off its podium. Man is designed and destined to live before an altar, the only question is whom or what sits there. It was a devastating realization that the one man whom for me had begun to encapsulate perfection should let me down. He represented the film world because in my eyes he had everything it was about: inspired ideas, creative flare, radical philosophies, good looks, sex appeal, hip dress sense, and every film producer, writer and media company pining after him. All this and yet when I casually asked him one Friday evening in a pub what his plans for the weekend were he replied in a facetious and off-hand tone, "Well I'm not going to a country house like you no doubt." As quick as a flash I was transported back to my primary school play ground and suddenly my whole world seemed meaningless.

My world had become about people like him and suddenly he was just a normal guy, if a little sad, insecure and chippy. If he was capable of making comments like that then what was I doing devoting my entire life to pleasing him? I had lost sight and perhaps had never really arrived at an understanding of why I was working in the film industry. I realised it wasn't really film that was in my blood. I wasn't in film for the sake of it, I was clearly looking for something else. Sure, despite being relatively underpaid, it was an okay way of earning money, and really fun at times, but I sensed my soul thirsting after something more. So, the icing on the cake arrived following a row with my boss following which I was 'encouraged to take a break' and went on holiday to Mallorca – as you do.

It seemed as though my job always left me dissatisfied. And in a way I realised at that moment that since university my life had revolved around my career. I have always been blessed with friends and had many, longstanding old friends. My social life felt like a given, it wasn't going anywhere and didn't need to, so I had invested this part of my life with copious hours in the workplace in order to get everything nailed down as it should be – to be a success in the eyes of the world. Sure, I was into women, but despite every romantic intention of developing a loving relationship, I seemed intrinsically incapable of getting beyond the physical. The truth is I had begun to worship certain women, mainly those I couldn't get with, whilst treating others as a means of sexual relief. The root was a broken heart, self-hatred and fear of intimacy, the potting soil, pornography and carnal lust.

CHAPTER 3
"COME HOME"

True idol

In the summer of 2002, aged twenty-six, a number of rickety old paths converged. My career was looking patchy, for the simple reason that the workplace no longer inspired me, relationships with women were dysfunctional and the fun of caning it every night had long since passed its sell by date. My acrimonious departure from the streets of Soho, in more ways than one, warranted and brought about on my part some deep reflection for the first time in my life.

What really was the point of any of it? It always seemed to be about me and what I could get. What was the point of me? Why was I even here? Why was I on earth? What was the point of anything? All these questions just came at me in a flurry. It was as though once the distractions of the aforementioned had been taken away there was nowhere else to hide. I had to try and find out. So in the summer of 2002 I set out to try and find the answer, the truth to life. Saturday November 23rd 2002 was to become the most important day of my life.

Okay. So what about religion? Surely Darwin had murdered God years ago? Surely in the age of the electric light bulb anything that conflicted with rational thought was pie in the sky? Religion was irrational, it seemed only to provoke division and killing and had never done anything for me in the past. It was either man's attempt to feel good about the world or to control it. A sort of feel good invention for life's losers who needed dogma or a crutch. And it was all about rules and it was boring as well. Well, I wasn't a loser, I wasn't boring and I didn't like rules. Or so I thought . . .

But who was this Jesus? Who was this Jesus whom this particularly pretty friend named Alice had recently confessed to 'follow'. Why would this perfectly sweet and intelligent girl with whom I had always agreed concerning the smugness and aggression of evangelical Christianity suddenly become a born again Christian? As far as I knew that only happened to naive, unintelligent people with little going for them. And why did I have to really fancy her right now and therefore have to look into doing that swear word course 'Alpha'?

Sure, Jesus is arguably the most famous person who ever walked the earth. It was only right that I should be able to write more than one could fit on a postage stamp about him, but why did I sense that He was the place to start? So I secretly enrolled on an Alpha course at my local church and was delighted to discover that I was the youngest in my 'small group' by at least ten years. This meant that I could distance myself somewhat from my fellow 'seekers' and not have to see in them my reflection – what I had come to think of as a slightly sad searching for meaning in life that clearly indicated personal weakness.

Conversely, I was also rather proud of myself on two accounts, such is the tragic irony. First, I was 'taking on' the course that many of my peers seemed scared to go on for fear of indoctrination and secondly I was re-embarking on the admirable journey of intellectual enlightenment that had alluded me for a good few years.

Wednesday evening pilgrimage

I remember loving Alpha. I would look forward to it all week. I just loved chewing over the meaty issues of life, discussing life and death, evolution, purpose, ethics, science, the supernatural – you name it. If it was profound then I had an opinion and I wanted it heard and listened to. I wanted my questions answered and more often than not I found that they weren't so much answered as new questions arose and old opinions, some of which I had lived by for years, just died.

I started to read voraciously around the subject and thrived in this gracious arena in which I was encouraged to mouth off as much as I wanted to. I started to like the people in my group and care about what they thought and what had happened in their lives. It was just so interesting. It felt like real life again, for the first time in years.

The mood of the place and the 'Alpha team' conjured up another interesting paradox, the paradox of course being something that I have become wonderfully aware of in recent years. On the one hand the seraphic smiley faces were out in force and jarred with my moody and proud scepticism, but on the other hand I came to appreciate the tangible sense of goodwill and generosity that flowed throughout the evening.

The course was free, the food was surprisingly good and we were waited upon hand and foot. I didn't lift a finger and despite having the opportunity to contribute a suggested and meagre donation for food, my wallet remained comfortably at the base of my pocket, as it had done in church for most of my life. Church and money were a non-sequitur and as far as I was concerned I was still doing them a favour by turning up.

The Alpha course opened my eyes to questions I suppose I had been wilfully avoiding for many years. If there is a God how would He show Himself? What is love and why do we need it? What happens when we die and can we know? Does atheism work? Is there a point to life, a point that transcends human existence? Can Christianity be looked at rationally and intelligently and not just with babyish, rose-tinted glasses?

I remember being slowly captivated by the person of Jesus as the weeks progressed. It was as though He started to live and breathe the more I heard and read about Him. He was a hero and He was real. He wasn't just a softee, He was tough and He did get nailed to a cross and die. That was a historical fact, as far as we can appreciate any historical fact. Why? Why did that happen and why had He had such a frighteningly dramatic impact on the world? He was frightening and beautiful. He was so wise and humble. He became intoxicating to me.

This person from whose birth we measure time and history. This person, the only person, who has ever claimed to be the Son of God and actually bothered to back it up with selflessness, world changing wisdom, miracles and resurrection from the dead. It's a big claim isn't it, to say 'Anyone who has seen me has seen the Father' (John 14:9)? It was a claim which started to jar. It jarred because I saw so much truth in Him, in His teaching, that it made me feel uneasy that He would lie, or indeed those writing about Him would lie (most of whom were executed for what they believed through witness, not just faith), about the things that seemed more and more unbelievable to me. Jesus said: ' I am the resurrection and the life, he who believes in Me will live, even though he dies.' (John 11 v 25) It didn't make sense that these beautiful stories, drenched in truth and love, should be underpinned by what was essentially a big lie and a con.

I had spent most of my life quite comfortable in the view that Jesus was a great moral teacher and maybe divinely anointed in some kind of cosmic way. But He was still just a man. Now I was faced with what some people have termed 'The Jesus problem'. As C.S. Lewis writes, 'A man who was merely a man and said the sort of things Jesus said would not be a great moral teacher.' He would either be insane or else he would be the 'Devil of Hell.' 'You must make your choice,' he writes. Either Jesus was, and is, the Son of God or else he was insane or evil but, C.S. Lewis goes on, 'let us not come up with any patronizing nonsense about His being a great human teacher. He has not left that open to us. He did not intend to.'

But maybe it wasn't about Jesus being a liar or insane? Maybe we should just leave Him out of it? After all, Jesus never put pen to paper. Maybe the Gospel writers were the ones who should take the blame? One big fantasy had been at play all along, the conspiracy to end all conspiracies. But that argument didn't sit with me for long either. The atheist John Stewart Mill asked this very important question: "Who among Jesus' disciples was capable of inventing the sayings ascribed to Jesus? Or imagining the life and character revealed in the gospels? Jesus seems to have a character so original, so complete, so uniformly consistent, so human and yet so far above human greatness that is it really possible to regard Him as a fraud or a fiction? It might be said that it would take more than a Jesus to actually invent a Jesus."

CHAPTER 4
"I AM THE DOOR"

Proper surrender

The Alpha weekend away quickly approached. Despite my increased enjoyment of the course, I had come to dread the weekend. I revered it as the weekend of change, the moment when the Demon Headmaster would say 'loooook intooo myyyy eyeeees chiiiiild.' I would leave on the Friday in a pair of Adidas trainers, smoking a fag, and return on the Sunday wearing a pair of those awful walking boots with a vacuous grin on my face.

By this stage I had started to see the point of the cross. I had caught the slightest glimpse of what it might mean to be forgiven for my sins and what this might mean to a Holy God. If God is holy, if God is love, then maybe my sin might be a problem. Maybe sin and evil in the world had a point, in the divine scheme of things? I realised that I had done stuff that had hurt people and hurt myself (and maybe God) and I guess it made sense that perhaps Jesus on the cross would provide an answer.

Maybe life without sin, or at least turned away from sin, might be the life that God had intended? I just remember having this gentle conviction that perhaps it all made sense. So despite every excuse to miss the weekend away, I went, wearing middle of the range loafers and determined to adopt an ambivalent, carefree approach to all that was thrown my way.

The thing is, it was quite understandable that I feared the weekend because it revolved around understanding and experiencing the person of the Holy Spirit. As far as my cereal packet Theology would stretch, this meant the power of God here on earth.

The Holy Spirit is God's way of touching us physically, emotionally, spiritually you name it – MOVING on earth. I agreed with all the teaching that I had heard about the church denying, forgetting about or sidelining the Holy Spirit. My experience of church had indeed been God the Father-focused, with a little bit of Jesus and next to no mention or allowance of the Holy Spirit. I had never seen any supernatural power in church. But that didn't mean I was ready for the real thing or indeed ready to know for certain that there wasn't any power in God on earth. I had always been safe in the hope that God might be there, if worst came to the worst. Surely If I asked him to move and then he didn't it would be generally worse than if I just trundled along for another ten years in blissfully hopeful ignorance albeit with a slightly more informed half faith that I could share at intellectual dinner parties.

As the weekend progressed these thoughts and feelings tossed about in my mind like smalls in a tumble dryer. At lunch time on the Saturday I remember fighting with my vicar, mentally not physically you might be relieved to hear, over the issue of pride and how it was a cop-out to be a Christian – it was the easy option. Yet clearly it was difficult to relinquish control? I was at the stage where intellectually I was there, I was sold, but the idea of being a Christian still made me feel sick. It was a cop-out to admit needing help and forgiveness and would mean that I would have to attach a metaphorical sign to my forehead, in pink neon, that alternately flashed 'looser/crutch boy' to the whole world. I realise now of course that we all have a crutch. People tell me Christianity is a crutch for needy people. Yes. What's yours?

We all have a crutch. The question is what? It's the way we're built. We're built to need God and if we don't choose and put our trust in Him we'll simply prop ourselves up on something fake. And fall over a lot, eventually for all eternity. The Bible calls this 'idolatry'. Jesus opened His most famous speech with the words "Blessed are the poor in spirit" – ie. happy are you if you're needy for Me. Neediness, desperation for spiritual satisfaction through Jesus is the foundation of the blessed, or happy, life.

Furthermore, Charles Marnham, my vicar, replied with a thought that was to be instrumental in my shift in attitude and continues to hold more and more truth to this day. He explained that on the contrary life as a Christian was increasingly difficult in this day and age and that it was anything but the easy option.

I had failed to see how I was contradicting myself. Yes, I had failed to spot another paradox. On the one hand the world often sees Christians as people who take the easy root, who are 'needy', but on the other hand, in their doing so it's made anything but easy to be one. Alice Cooper illustrates the point amusingly: 'Even the addicts are saying, "It doesn't matter how many drugs I take, I'm not fulfilled. This isn't satisfying." There's a spiritual hunger going on. Everybody feels it. If you don't feel it now, you will. Trust me. You will . . . Drinking beer is easy. Trashing your hotel room is easy. But being a Christian, that's a tough call. That's rebellion.'

As I walked off my nervy and meagre ploughman's lunch I remember laughing on the telephone with Dave, a friend of mine, about how our group was about to ask the Holy Spirit to come and that when he next saw me I would be a changed man. Despite my propensity for sarcasm and the cynical embers that remained nestled within my wounded character, I did genuinely believe that something big was about to happen. I felt it in my spirit.

Jump

That Saturday afternoon, in a parochial, converted barn thirty miles outside of London, I prayed 'the prayer'. I prayed from the bottom of my heart for the first time in my adult life. I thanked God for Jesus and for the cross, I asked for forgiveness, and really meant it, and asked to be filled with God's Holy Spirit.

It's funny; because looking back I remember very nearly not praying anything. I had a clear choice and my first decision was 'no'. It was as though I didn't want to take the risk. My feeling was that I would leave it a while and maybe think about it some more. You see, I was jostling with issues of self-identity still and was worried that God would change me into some sort of preaching freak who never had any fun (no irony intended). But then I remember recognising this typical attitude that I had adopted for so long now. This kind of non-committal, diluted, easy approach to my life, a life which in so many ways carried less and less meaning. I realised that I never committed properly to anything. There was always a caveat, a get out clause, and most importantly an escape route for D.L. Muir Esq., the master of his own destiny.

So I took a hold of myself and followed my heart.

I knew that I was really saying to God, 'If you're there, I'm yours'. If God existed He knew this prayer was real. He knew that if nothing happened beyond a sort of mental and academic acceptance of a religion, that pretty soon I would be off for good.

On November 23rd 2002 the Holy Spirit filled my heart and body. At the risk of sounding trite and irreverent I am loathe to put into words what God does to you when He tells you He loves you, that He is real and that He has been there for you, waiting, all along. It is different for everyone and transcends the capability of the English language, or at least certainly my use of it. But I know you can't wait to know all the details, and God knows I'm irreverent – so here goes.

The Reverend Charles Marnham gently led proceedings from in front of the fireplace. We comprised a group of about ten 'heavenly candidates'. We were asked to bow our heads in prayer and hold our hands out in front of us if we wanted to receive prayer from the prayer ministry team with 'the laying on of hands', an act which we were reassured was typically biblical. Proud, self-conscious and suspicious of the supernatural, I adopted a position at the back of the room, hands firmly at my sides, and simply closed my eyes.

I prayed the prayer in silent words from my mind and my heart. Within thirty seconds, in the quiet of the room, a hand was gently laid upon my shoulder and at that very moment electric waves of liquid love, peace, joy and intense heat flooded through my body, soul and spirit. I was left in no doubt that the God of the Universe had visited me personally. The strength in my legs left suddenly and years of pent up emotion scrambled to the surface, as though a dam in my soul had finally been violently overcome. I choked back tears proudly. Then the hand was removed and the power lifted.

To this day I don't know whose hand it was. Perhaps it belonged to an angel, perhaps Jesus Himself. It wouldn't be the first time and certainly not the last. According to Charles, whom I inquired upon at a later date, the prayer ministry team was otherwise engaged and had been firmly instructed only to lay hands on those who asked.

Within seconds the hand alighted once again on my shoulder in the same gentle manner. Again tremendous supernatural power, love and fire cascaded through everything that is Dominic. In a second I knew I had been made uniquely, that God knew me and loved me intensely and that I was part of His plan here and beyond. It felt like my heavenly Father was smiling down at me and saying, "I've been here all along, I'm so glad you've come." I continued to stifle the tears and ensured that any collapse from my incapacitated body was prevented by a semi-dignified slump on to a neighboring sofa.

I got myself outside and by myself as quickly as I could. I walked out into a world that Someone had made and that was being looked down upon. I half expected to see a canopy in the sky that God was looking through – like that film 'The Truman Show'. It was that bizarre. Totally different. Like black and white to colour, dark to light. Small birds darted around the autumn sky and sung joyfully. They too had been created lovingly and had a purpose. I hardly said a word to anyone for several hours. Communication was frivolous, nay irreverent. On the way home I saw a magpie by itself sitting on a telegraph pole. A victim of superstition, normally I would have saluted it feverishly lest its solitude bring immediate and guaranteed sorrow into my life. This time I just smiled gleefully, overjoyed and truly free for the first time in my life.

CHAPTER 5
"LET'S HAVE SOME FUN"

Life in the kingdom

The next day, a Sunday, I turned up for church early. It was more exciting than going to a movie premiere or a trendy, guest-list-imperative nightclub. I'm not joking. It wasn't so much about the building, more the thought that I might meet Him again, feel His touch.

The church service was delicious and rich with meaning and purpose. I'd spent years and years bored by the words on any service sheet. Now I examined them and they made me feel good. They were about Him. In the past I'd found church tedious in the extreme, except when someone farted or tripped over and then it was suffocatingly funny.

But really, in church I had always been a clock-watcher. Now the thing just wasn't long enough. Next, I joined a weekly Bible study where I was the youngest by twenty years. I was early to that too. Anything to do with God and I was there. I couldn't help myself, it felt good, He felt good, and life was the best thing ever. As the weeks went by I would get hit with waves of joy and revelation of Him at the most random times.

Several months later, in the late spring of 2003 I decided to start praying about my job. I was kind of busting out of the religious notion of only praying for the poor and other people, as important as that is at the right time. I'd learned a thing or two about Jesus, His love for me and the genuine interest He had in my seemingly insignificant life. The religious, orphan-hearted stronghold was beginning to come down I'm pleased to say! Besides, if prayer was going to work for me it had to be enjoyable, so I figured if I prayed about things that would directly impact my life so that I could see answers then my relationship with God would strengthen.

In a sense I was giving my career to God, testing the water to see if He had any bright ideas. My faith and love for Him was growing daily and I suppose I had reached a level of excitement and trust where I wanted to cut Him some more slack. The more you get to know God and his goodness the more you want to give to Him and see Him move. He's wonderfully addictive in that way.

God began to woo me with answers to prayer, fresh attitudes and blasts of joy! To get another God buzz you have to get where He is. I was praying that He would guide me into the right job. I also threw in a clause on 'excitement'. I wanted something challenging and exciting. I was teaching at the time, and making short films and wedding videos. I was perfectly happy, whatever that really means, but felt in my spirit that there had to be more.

A few weeks later I received a telephone call one afternoon whilst sat at my desk writing school reports. It was from a friend of mine named Dave (the same one who phones before something big is going to happen) asking whether I'd like to be contacted by a television production company regarding a PBS/Channel 4 project called 'Colonial House' (the English version is called 'Pioneer House'). It transpired that they were looking for English men in their twenties to participate in a history based reality television project!

I gave Dave the green light and was called within about ten minutes by a Production Manager named Emma. The next day I was interviewed and given a test screening and within about two weeks I was down to the last three and was on a plane to Boston to be met by the American team. I got the part and another two weeks later I was in remote Massachusetts, US, being trained in tree felling, animal slaughter and sea fishing amongst many other bizarre and exciting seventeenth century pursuits. Another Brit named Paul accompanied me and alongside fourteen Americans we were equipped to spend five months 'in the year 1628'.

That's how quickly everything happened. I felt like God had to be in this. It had fallen out of the sky and seemed too ironic for words. One minute I was slightly stifled by my job and the heat of the London summer and the next I was stripped down to one set of period clothing and my Bible. All in the cause of spending five months cut off from everything and everyone I ever knew to live as a 'Pilgrim Father' for twenty million people to see.

God is good, but he's not "safe", at least with our stifflling comfort zone. In truth, his will is the safest place for us. But be prepared if you are going to test Him on his sense of humour and adventure.

1628 Colonial life was, for me, about nature, simplicity and God. I couldn't help feeling part of this organic, natural melting pot. It's so easy to say that one feels part of nature – it's one of the great cliché's. When other people say this it usually sounds odious to me and I always roar with laughter when it's used facetiously in Woody Allen films. But I remember my clothes gradually became a new layer of skin - clothes that were made of wool and linen. They became embroiled with dirt, sweat, wood chippings and smoke and I would often find pebbles in my pockets.

Having milked the goats or cleaned out their pen, both distinctly unsavory chores, I would sleep in my milk-stained clothes and rarely wash my hands. It was almost as though the dirt on your hands became clean. It was clean dirt, if that makes sense, it just lived with you and you in it. No, that's not an oxymoron. You had to be there. Get the DVD.

The animals were such a central part of our lives, and our respective domiciles left so little to differentiate us, that our humanity was forced to find new realms of expression – often without success. By the time I had stacked wood next to our hearth and collected water for the evening a new skin would have arrived, many natural textures would have come and gone. If I wasn't in contact with wood, in the handle of an axe, a tree trunk or a hand-carved bowl, I was foraging around in the bushes and the dirt or straightening my woollen doublet or an errant goat. Even going to the loo was about scoping the land, digging with wooden tools, and pruning near by vegetation. I'll pause the New Age soundtrack right here to allow your imagination to wander.

My life on the Colony was simple. I went to bed with the sun and got up with the cockerel. I would concentrate on eating as much porridge and 'peas pottage' as I could, not worrying too much about taste, but would ensure I had enough energy for the work. Food was like petrol, if you didn't eat enough you conked out and had to go to bed. For the first few weeks this happened to many of us regularly.

I chopped wood, carried it, and made it do things, or at least tried to. Sometimes I fished and often I read the Bible — they were my distractions and became my passions. Remember that the only book we were allowed was the Bible. In 1628, that's pretty much all anyone had! I had prayed a prayer for God to move on my life. I had prayed for something exciting to happen. Now I was living in a time warp in remote New England, wearing seventeenth century clothes, away from everything I had ever known. However, I had met God a few months earlier and surely He was with me?

Surely there was reason somewhere for all this madness?

CHAPTER 6
"THE THREE-COURSE MEAL"

I really like food. For many years, this has been thoroughly catered for by the endowment of an athletic metabolism. Food is a very good invention. Milk puddings, melted cheese, mayonnaise, bacon, chips and sausages are favourites that spring to mind right now. On the colony we had to ration butter and three prunes a week was our 'special treat'. I was the resident Quarter Master so at least I got to enjoy a sense of power and favour in dealing out our meager supplies.

The love of food, at least its consumption (it's staggering how much time we spent torturously talking about it) had to take a back seat. So instead I started to eat the word of God! It tasted good. I didn't really understand why, in the past it had dragged mercilessly, but now it was living. I think it was living because it somehow connected me with Him. It became a conversation. A conversation that would feed my soul, in a way that other conversations had failed.

If I read the Bible with the intention of connecting with Him, to meet Him, then that's what happened. If I read it as just a book, then nothing – dull. I began to realise that it's not about a book, it's about a Person. It's not about a church building, it's about a Person. It's not about a set of life-robbing rules, it's about a life-giving relationship.

Whenever I read little slices of my Bible, I met Him. Whenever I took little bites, my soul felt bigger, stronger, more 'buzzy'. Do you believe God invented that buzzy bit in our make-up? I was only just beginning to realise that it wasn't just invented for Class-A drugs, or even romantic love but that actually God wanted to inhabit it Himself. St Augustine said 'Our heart is restless until it rests in thee.' I had known that to be true of my life before meeting Jesus. Now that I knew Him, I was beginning to see its outworking every day. If I didn't get Jesus, I felt restless. Only in Him, when we spent time together, were things cool, peaceful and fulfilled. Wild, huh? It still blows my mind.

God tasted good (Psalm 34:8). God was an experience, a meal for my soul, more still, God was like having dinner with a friend. Could God be a three-course meal? After all He's the Godhead right – the Trinity? Three-in-one, one-in-three etc? I didn't know the Holy Spirit at this stage. Yes, I'd met Him on that Alpha weekend, but I thought that this was a one off meeting and that my one token was used up at 'salvation'. Like I'd managed to pick up his autograph but should probably frame it and gaze wistfully at it for the rest of my life. Annoyingly, I didn't know that you could hang out with the Holy Spirit and, if you wanted, soak in His glorious, loving, supernatural presence all day, every day. This was aeons away from the distant and moody God I'd conceived of at Catholic mass, Anglican Evensong and all the 'churchy' places I'd grown up around.

This is what God wants for His children more than anything. He wants to just hang with us. God is our Father also and He created us specifically to be in relationship with Him. Good, earthly fathers long to spend time with their kids. They don't just set them to task, make them jump through hoops and wait to catch them making a hash of things. What must our heavenly Father, the only perfect Father, really be like? (Matthew 5:48)

That said, looking back, had I known this revelation of 'soaking' in the presence of the Holy Spirit and speaking in tongues, whilst out in the middle of remote New England, I might have got myself in trouble! At the time I knew enough to know the gentle and pleasant touch of God, and that, in itself, was perfect.

God and I were beginning to make friends.

In the evening before bed I would drink a pint of beer and maybe consult my Quarter Master ration book. As the sun dipped below the horizon occasionally my opinion on a colony matter would be asked for or maybe I would just shoot the breeze with a friend. Then I would go to bed and sleep soundly only to repeat the simplicity day after day.

Slowly but surely I became aware of God more and more. The faith I took with me into the project was strong but more convenient to a busy London schedule. Slowly He started to walk with me and I with Him. He would be there and I would welcome His presence and ask Him to reveal Himself more and more. And He did. In the waving trees or the freezing water He was there in His glory. I think it is very easy to say 'creation is my church', or to constantly relate nature to God. All that is great and needs to happen more, particularly where dead religious ritual prevails. But there's a danger in going to the other extreme. There is clearly a distinction between worshipping the creation and worshipping the Creator.

When I say I felt His presence in the trees, I mean it. But I was looking for His heart. I would feel His manifest, tangible presence. God's artwork, His 'nature expression', rather than being an end in themselves, provided a conduit into His heart and His personality. Often, alongside a glance at the rustling leaves, my spirit would receive a heavenly, supernatural download. I didn't know at the time that this was the Holy Spirit. I would sense His love pour down on me when I thought about the rain's journey. I was still learning that God wants us to feel His presence.

Human beings need touch, we are built that way. God wants to cuddle us, and that's why He has given us His Holy Spirit (Romans 5:5). He wants us to want Him in this way. It's okay to want to feel Him. In the Psalm 63, King David speaks of his soul longing for God, his flesh crying out for the living God.

Every Sunday we had a Colonial style Sabbath church service led by the resident Lay Preacher. It was fun to get together in this way and provided fascinating historical insight into the history of the church. However, it was in the quiet of steady labour or the isolation of a hike into the wild that I would meet with Jesus.

When your soul is quietened and brought into rest, all heaven breaks loose in your spirit!

I also began to recognise Jesus in the community that we managed to build. There was a palpable love in that colony, in spite of and no doubt arising from the many difficulties shared, and He was in it.

Oprah Winfrey (far left) visited and stayed in our Colony. Oprah was in the congregation during my first ever preach. (That's me, second from the right)

Heart Changer

'I had a mixed weekend and fell out with a guy (the carpenter) who I live with and like. If you have a row here life becomes unbearable. I was ready to quit but I prayed to God to help me and everything has been sorted out. He is my constant saviour out here.'

> (Extract from a quill-penned letter sent to my parents, 'by ship', on the 21st of July!)

During that five month experience on the colony God became my saviour, best friend and miracle maker. He was the only one with me always. He was the only one who knew what was going on in my heart. He was the only one who could actually do something to help me.

On two occasions I seriously considered leaving the project to return to England. I remember going for a long walk and breaking down in tears of confusion over what to do. I felt totally alone. I barely knew anyone and no one knew anything about me so seeking decent, practical advice was next to impossible. I informed the production crew that I was seriously considering leaving the project and needed to contact friends or family in England in order to get some perspective but they promptly reminded me that it was forbidden to have any outside contact.

I had come to the end of myself. Little did I appreciate the benefit of such a place! So I got down on my knees at the top of a rocky hill and cried out to God. I told Him, out loud through snotty sobs, that I felt it had been His will to bring me on this absurd TV show and that He would have to do something pretty massive to get me out of this dilemma and keep me here, if that's what He wanted.

With that I loped back to the colony, drenched in doubt and self-pity, and flung myself into bed mid afternoon. I don't think I have ever been to bed so early in the day with the unqualified intention of sleeping through to the next day.

The next morning I woke with a joyful sense of purpose. I absolutely knew that I was meant to be on that Colony. I was happy and at peace. Not only that, but I was instilled with fresh vision and determination. It was as though I had been given a totally new heart and mind. I had done nothing, I had merely been asleep, but don't try telling me that I just 'slept it off'. You should have seen me the day before! I was a wreck. Now I felt like William Wallace, complete with navy war paint and mullet, ready to take back the bonnie land.

This miraculous 'emotional deliverance', for want of a better expression, happened twice during that long summer. I had secretly suspected that the point of this television extravaganza was that God would thrust me into the media limelight and tickle that much-hallowed dream of being famous, but for His purposes of course. Not entirely surprisingly, He had a different agenda – friendship and fun with Himself (although I did get interviewed on the 'Richard and Judy Show' which mildly appeased my now waning craving).

I've learned that God will often draw us to Himself by appealing to our likes and weaknesses, just so that he can give us something far better. God knows us more intricately than we know ourselves and I'm pleased to say has the upper hand. He knows what he has to work with!

America was God's cunning way of showing me the walk of relationship with Him. It appeared that restored relationship with God was the whole point of the cross. 'Christianity', that badly packaged taboo, wasn't about rules, judgement, and boredom with a slice of 'no fun'. The cross of Jesus was about exciting, perilous and adventurous relationship with the God of the universe.

God used a seventeenth century colony to begin dealing with my brokenness, destructive habits and harmful attitudes. 'Sin' was a word that at last began to carry significant and powerful meaning. God was giving me a shower and a clean up in a place where there was no shower. I stank on the outside but I was beginning to smell better on the inside. It was such a relief to feel cleaner. I began to feel more free and enter new realms of peace every day. I learned that God is tough, that walking his way was tricky, it was narrow (Matthew 7:13-14). It seemed He was too loving to be easy on me but always gentle in the process. He had a plan. He was too holy to be complicit with me and too majestic to make things comfortable. God was "tough", yet kind, fascinating, wild and loving all at the same time.

God's ways seem to hurt at times, the journey isn't easy but every time I come through the short-lived pain I seem to say 'thank you, you know best!'. I know that sounds weird. You have to see for yourself (Hebrews 12:5-11). 'Christianity' wasn't about 'going to church', as I had always feared, but about being God's friend, His son, and walking through life together and into more life.

CHAPTER 7
"I'LL TURN UP THE POWER NOW"

Once seventeenth century life had finished with me I returned to London and very quickly enrolled on another 'Alpha' course. Again, I found myself on the 'Holy Spirit weekend' in a seaside hotel in Brighton. We gathered together on the Sunday morning to call on the Holy Spirit in order to give Him a chance to minister to us all. What followed was the most powerful exposure to God's working and moving that I had witnessed in my life to that day.

As I have explained, for years as an agnostic and then faithless atheist, I would patronizingly condescend to Christians, often remarking on their faith in such terms as 'that's good for you' or 'I'm glad that it makes you happy, but it's not for me.' This attitude owed largely to the fact that I had simply never seen any supernatural power, any evidence of an Almighty God, whenever I'd been in church.

From a distance the gospel story was implausible and sadly my worldly wisdom was never close to being confounded by the 'awesome' power of God, documented in parts of the Bible. 'Awesome' was just a word I used to describe a decent movie or left-footed volley from outside the box. I had understandably consigned those weird supernatural parts of the Bible, in Ezekiel and Revelation etc, to myth.

Unknowingly I had spent years carefully fashioning my own, rather neat, harmless and entirely false understanding of Christianity.

What I experienced that day in Brighton, however, was far from harmless. It was electrifying, life-changing and ecstatic. After a short time of worship, the 'clappy' guitar and band sort (to which I was slowly warming), we all cleared away the chairs excitedly in preparation for God to come. I mean, how cool is that?

Readying a room, commonly used for local Bingo events, for a fresh outpouring of the Spirit of Almighty God! This was real church. The room was filled with nervous anticipation as we each carefully picked a spot to stand in. There must have been a hundred and fifty of us. Some people chose to be inconspicuous at the back of the room, (I could sympathize), whilst others just threw themselves into the middle of the floor, in a kind of seasoned, 'show me the money' kind of way. I noticed a nervous agnostic friend file surreptitiously out of a side exit.

The Reverend John Peters called on the Holy Spirit to come. Within about three minutes I was engulfed in ecstatic supernatural power, much like I had experienced a year previously in that converted barn, but this time it was stronger and for a prolonged period of time. Over a period of about thirty minutes I had to be held up by two men as wave after wave after wave of liquid love and supernatural power swept through my body.

I was overheating, sweating, shaking, but I wanted more. I wanted more of him. I knew He was filling me, the Holy Spirit of God was upon me, and so naturally why would I put on the brakes? My head was thrust back to face the ceiling by surges of power, my back arched back precariously also, and my soul was exploding with life. It's very difficult to describe without doing God an injustice, not for the first time. But I want to testify to the truth as best I can.

The important thing to stress is this: you know it's God when it happens. It is a feeling unlike anything else on earth and meets a need that only one's designer could have accommodated for. It seemed as though every longing that my life had ever had was met in this one encounter. Every craving satisfied (John 7:37-39). Finally there was peace and fulfillment in my innermost being.

It's the same today. Nothing can satisfy the longing in my heart but Him on a daily basis. That's the way we are made. And my God I believe in Him when it happens, when I meet and hang out with His Spirit. My God I fall in love with Him every time. Every day I come to God to get filled with life, love, faith and supernatural power. That's normal Christianity. The Bible says we love Him because He first loved us.

That Sunday morning in November 2003 I was meeting this tangible, personal love for the second time in my life. Forget religious striving: trying to be holy, trying to pass tests, trying to please God; I was tasting grace. This was the start of a beautiful relationship with the Holy Spirit of God. You need to meet God, you can't just read about Him. He has made the provision, on that bloody cross, for every human being to meet Him personally before death. That's the start of salvation. Nothing less.

God is a supernatural God who wants to touch His children and show us how real He is. This is the 'born again' experience. There's no other type of Christian than a 'born again Christian', 'new creation' one, whichever variation on that theme you want to use (John 3:7, 1 Peter 1:23). That's not my opinion, that's what the Bible says. I'm less interested in man's take on salvation or Christianity, I want God's. Man picks what suits him and don't I know it in my self. Jesus, the Son of God, says you must be born again. We need to get over it, the label, the pride, fear, whatever. There's a reason the world is scared of 'born again Christians' – it's because they are convicted of the Truth. We're labelled 'too nutty', 'over zealous', 'in your face'. Well, let me assure you, as a former persecutor to this 'intolerable breed of Christian', they (we) are 'zealous' because we have had an encounter or series of encounters with the living God of the universe. You try remaining the same after that one. You try keeping your faith to yourself after that little fair ride! I dare you. Taste and see. Zeal for God is a beautiful thing.

For months afterwards I would taste of God's loving presence on a daily basis. In the bath, in bed, lying on the floor of my bedroom, sitting in the park, everywhere. It just amazed me that wherever I was He would come, that glorious, manifest presence. I had God on tap. We come to God boldly through the blood of

Jesus. The bible says that Jesus is the door, the only way. You can't have the presence of God without Jesus and the cross. Put another way, you can't have the kingdom of God without the gospel. It is important to stress that because you can access the spiritual realm in a number of ways, but only one way, the Way, Jesus, is safe – but I'll explain more about that later on.

I would endeavour to confess any sin to him, clear my conscience, and just ask his Spirit to come. I couldn't get enough of him. I was 'in church' the whole time! It was glorious. The reality is that I was learning the meaning of church. I was church, because I was a temple of the Holy Spirit; I could feel Him inside me (1 Corinthians 6:19).

Like I explained earlier, and I don't think this point can be overstated (Lord, forgive a few hundred years of dead Christianity) I had thought church was a building, a slightly austere and ritualistic place of religion. I was learning in greater and greater depths that 'church' is a relationship with a living, loving, supernatural God, not a religion. 'Church' is the body of Christ, the people who house 'the Spirit of Christ' coming together in community! Church is living, loving, supernaturally powerful and adventurous beyond measure - it certainly ain't confined to four walls.

When me and my friends 'do church' we take that divine relationship, that supernatural power and love out into the streets and change the world. 'Churchianity' was something I grew up around, totally lacking in life, love and power. It was dead religion. Christianity was not about religion. God hates dead religion. Jesus never intended to start a religion, He came to the earth to establish a kingdom, the kingdom of God (Matthew 6:9-10), and I was about to discover just how terrifyingly real this all was and the eternal implications for all of us.

CHAPTER 8
"YOUR TURN"

I couldn't get enough of God's presence. Could it be that the Holy Spirit couldn't get enough of me? He never let me down. He was always there, always faithful. Where was all this leading anyway? The more I tasted of His goodness, of His paradise, the more I would want Him. The more I wanted Him, the more I wanted others to know Him.

Within weeks of that experience in Brighton, what I refer to as my baptism in the Holy Spirit (Acts 1:5 – Acts 2), I felt a call to "full-time ministry". In September 2004 I was super blessed to be accepted as an intern at Holy Trinity Brompton, London. My hunger for God and to see Him move in and through my life was becoming insatiable. HTB was a wonderful place to grow in the things of the Kingdom of God and appreciate the many facets of church life. I made many new friends and even met the girl who would become my wife and mother to my son. The day I met Thea, as our hands touched for the first time, I felt in my spirit that she would be my wife. It would take a glorious, beautiful, complicated, miraculous, immensely painful twelve year journey to get us to the altar on our wedding day. We named our son Redemption, in honour of God's ways. (The full story is perhaps for another book in the future).

One afternoon after work at HTB I was locking up my bike outside my block of flats in Victoria, London, when I noticed Ronnie, a local street sleeper with two other seemingly homeless friends hanging out with him. At the time I lived right next to quite a prominent London hostel called 'The Passage', so to see clutches of homeless convening outside my door was not uncommon. I have met Ronnie a few times. He is always exceedingly inebriated and remarkably upbeat. He must be about mid-forties, well-built, well weathered and sports an impressively long goatee beard.

His hands are red and swollen and he talks and talks. It is difficult to get a word in edge ways.

Ronnie took to the streets and to alcoholism when his wife died of cancer. He has something like five children whom he sees from time to time. It just so happened that I had one of those amazing trays of Krispy Kreme doughnuts from Harrods on me, albeit with only three remaining. Something told me that these three needed them more than me so I thought I'd go over and drop them off and say 'Hi'. It was a freezing afternoon and actually the sight of the doughnuts did little to stir their enthusiasm. I hopped around for a few minutes trying to stay warm in my North Face, goose down Parker coat, wondering whether I could be of any use to these guys.

The truth is I had not planned this. I said a quick prayer to God asking Him to use me, asking Him for some way in here. I never usually get anywhere with Ronnie, in terms of the Gospel, normally we just chat about life, its sorrows and his 'Godfather' role on the streets. He sees himself, as it seems do all that meet him, as a protecting, almost mentoring force for good on the streets. He is proud of his purpose and role.

On this afternoon it looked as though he was quite happy chatting with the girl sitting on his right (she must have been mid twenties) and a French guy called Robert who was standing on my left. Ronnie was well gone, the girl seemed pretty sober and Robert was between the two. It was quarter past three in the afternoon and I had some work at home to get on with. I started to gather up the doughnuts, frustrated at the thought that they would go to waste here (!) and at that moment Ronnie chirped up and assured me that they would come in handy later.

So at that stage I thought I would introduce myself to the French guy called Robert. It turned out he had been in London about six months and was pitifully addicted to Stella Artois – six cans in the morning and six cans in the afternoon. He was about thirty and sounded positive about a bed in a hostel he had only recently secured. His English was remarkably good, he looked pretty well and I was amazed to see him in this position in life. I asked him if he had any faith and he replied promptly in the affirmative that he was a Catholic. He had nothing else to add. I replied that I was a Catholic but that actually for a large part of my life it had remained only a label to me.

My spirit emboldened, I embarked on my story with God. I told him that I used to drink and take drugs a lot and that two or so years ago Jesus had come into my life and freed me from these needs. I told him confidently that I had spent most of my life not believing in God but that upon really seeking Him He had broken in suddenly and powerfully with his love and peace. And that I knew He existed, that Jesus is alive and that most importantly He loved me.

Robert looked unmoved and sceptical. He said that it was superficial and that any change in my habits was all 'in the mind'. He backed up his diagnosis by simultaneously tapping his head pointedly with his finger and engaging eye contact with me for nearly the first time. I replied authoritatively that there was nothing superficial about being filled with the Holy Spirit of God. In spite of his apparent unbelief Robert offered no reply. On the contrary I insisted that it had been the most profound and life changing day of my life.

He seemed a little more curious, indeed I had a sense that he was perhaps even intrigued albeit in that slightly self-effacing way. So I asked him casually if I might pray for him. He shrugged and said that that would be fine. So I put my hand on his shoulder, in the quiet of my mind asked God to give me a prayer, and just started a kind of blessing. I felt calm and Robert looked at peace. Out loud I just thanked God for our meeting, for Robert and for God's love for him. The prayer came naturally and simply. Both our eyes were open and Robert was looking into the distance. I could here Ronnie rabbiting on in the background, unaware of what was happening.

I then called on the Holy Spirit to come and fill Robert. And I waited.

I felt the Holy Spirit upon me and watched Robert carefully, as I knew that God was with us in power. I saw Robert manifest a reaction and his eyes twitched and he lurched ever so slightly. I told Robert that I sensed the power of God upon us and at that moment, he urgently reached for something in his pocket. As he struggled to release something from his jean pocket he just said "It's hot, it's hot", in a slightly bewildered fashion. He then looked at me and opened his hand to reveal a crucifix on a Catholic rosary chain. He said it was hot and with that he seemed to clasp it all the more dearly almost as if to warm both his hands and soul. We carried on praying and I sensed God speak to Robert.

He began to look more and more whimsical and moved. I could tell he was experiencing profound revelation. I felt that I should leave Robert to reflect at this stage. I sensed that he needed time to think and that I should get out of his face for a bit. Also, by this time Ronnie had cottoned on to the proceedings and was exclaiming noisily that 'the whole thing' was a 'load of bollocks'.

I gave Robert a leaflet, called 'Why Jesus?' which has the address of my church on it and answers the aforementioned question. I said that I lived right here and gave him my flat number should he need anything. I also pointed to a prayer at the back of the leaflet he might want to say by himself later. With that I left overjoyed and managed to catch Robert's eye one more time, with one of those bonding, mutually knowing looks, as I put my key into the door.

This was one of a few early encounters with lost people on the streets that would change my life irrevocably and scar me for street evangelism to this very day. I was beginning to understand that Jesus calls us not to pew-warming but hell-emptying. We are called to be fishers of men in the drowning sea of humanity-Christianity is not just a pleasure cruiser, it's a life boat.

CHAPTER 9
"NOW IT'S TIME TO MEET THE ENEMY"

God was becoming the supernatural God that I read about in the Bible; the miracle maker, the healer, the dancing hand of power at work through His people. I would read the gospels and marvel at how the life of Jesus was littered with supernatural encounters between two kingdoms – the kingdom of God and the kingdom of Darkness. But why was the average church experience still so predicitable and safe? In the summer of 2006 I realised I needed to stretch the envelope of my middle class, church-lite, comfort zone and embark on a short-term mission to India.

The Indian ride starts by exercising the natural senses. Upon exiting the plane one is hit by a plethora of smells, textures, wafts, colours, tastes and noises. Car horns hardly cease beeping, vegetable curry and rice is more common than beef in McDonalds, exuberant flowers and terracotta dust battle with fluorescent strip lighting, and someone's toilet never seems that far away – which is probably no bad thing for the neurotic English missionary, lacking faith in certain areas.

India is a weird and wonderful country. It is chaotic and charming, poor and hot. The moment Clive and I arrived we raced to our air-conditioned hotel room and passed out – jet lag, of course. Clive was a seasoned missionary, clearly, who spent the best part of a decade with his family in The Republic of Niger, an oasis of sorts in the Sahara desert with around 2,000 Christians and millions of Muslims. He had been through the 'spiritual mill' and come out the other end hardened and softened, I'd suggest in all the right places. He now evangelises in villages around the world and God heals people when the gospel has been preached. I had the amazing privilege of being Clive's bag carrier on this occasion. It's great, being someone like Clive's bag carrier – you get more than tanned biceps.

The first part of the trip was spent at a school for Prophets and the supernatural run by a powerful man of God named Ezekiah Francis. He is a Prophet of God, the sort of man who gets up on the stage without any notes and speaks for hours whilst you drink in every word bathing and then clothing yourself in truth. Scripture upon scripture flowed, corporate prophecy, personal prophecy. He also wept.

There were around five hundred Indians there for this twelve-day school, men and women, most ages. They all slept on the vast expanse that is a church floor and were up to worship at five in the morning. I joined them enthusiastically, cashing in on the hot weather and jet lag. On the second day Pauloses, an Indian apostle and our host, took us to a local Hindu pilgrimage. I figured this was a kind of sightseeing break from the real stuff, a chance to take a few snaps and reflect romantically upon Indian culture. Sure, the Hindu faith was clearly an alternative to the message of Christ, and in that sense one needed to be prepped up, but in my naivety I was ill prepared for the horrors that lay ahead.

Thousands of Indians, grouped in large families, thronged the extended locale of a large Hindu temple and its neighbouring river. Stalls and shops lined the dusty walkway, it felt a bit like being crammed into a music festival; either side large groups of people cooked over open fires, some camped out and there was a perpetual drum beat that pierced the ominous atmosphere.

Pauloses led us down to the river in order to explain to us what was happening. Pauloses must be in his late fifties. He grew up in a Hindu family. A rebellious teenager, he was in and out of prison before giving his life to Christ aged sixteen whereupon his Father booted him out of the house for his new professed faith. He now has a large family of his own and a prolific apostolic ministry across the nation of India having planted sixty-two churches and discipled many other apostles, some of whom have also planted upwards of ten churches.

Pauloses knows the meaning of suffering for Christ. He has been beaten within inches of his life on several occasions by Hindu radicals and has lived with his pregnant wife and family in a fish packing shed when there was nowhere else to go. Pauloses has just lived Jesus. He has seen how God can take a sold-out heart such as his and change thousands of lives. He has also seen the dead raised and had a personal visitation from the Lord Jesus Christ Himself. It's no wonder that upon meeting him one is struck by his fierce sturdiness and almost unnerving humility. Pauloses is a man under authority.

The river was punctuated with scores of flamboyantly-dressed families, from a distance like stepping stones made from piles of Smarties. Each family seemed to be huddled around the focal point, a chosen family member or members, bearing the offering to their spirit or god. According to Pauloses each family worships a separate spirit (there are millions of gods in Hinduism).

Pauloses explained that the first part of the ritual involved being washed from their sins in the water of the river. Once this is done the family call upon their spirit to come and then process in worship up to the nearby temple, circumnavigate it four times and then enter it to pledge their offering and worship.

On the bank of the teaming river in the baking morning sun I watched with a mixture of horror and pity as, in some cases teenage girls, became possessed with what could only be described as evil spirits. Their bodies would contort and their faces would be overtaken with pain and fear. Tears of sadness and resignation would search out the river. Their eyes glazed over and they became as the walking tortured or worse, dead.

In some horrifyingly dramatic cases, the family members carrying the offering, usually boasting impressive flames at this stage, would reel out of control and descend into uncontrollable fits on the dirt floor, writhing around like demented animals. Meanwhile some family members would attempt to gather them up whilst others danced, chanted and drummed their way to the temple. It was truly shocking and I was barely able to maintain objectivity with the camera as family upon family, a seemingly endless trail of suffering and fear, made their pilgrimage from the river.

With a determined expression worn by a man aggressively refreshed in his vocation, Pauloses informed me that this particular pilgrimage, allegedly a popular one, goes on for a week and more than a million Indian Hindus attend it. This privileged slice of 'sight-seeing', this VIP exposure to Hinduism, brought the gospel of Jesus Christ and his victory over the powers of darkness to life in a new and profound way.

> *"But if I drive out demons by the finger of God, then the kingdom of God has come to you."*
>
> Luke 11:20

It was only fitting that fewer than three nights later Clive and I found ourselves in the middle of the Indian scrub in a remote village preparing to preach the gospel. We were linked up with Mohan, the leader of one of Pauloses' church plants. Mohan and his team had incisively prepared for our arrival. They had hired PA, stage and lighting equipment for our tour of local villages and I think a bit of old-fashioned street crying had gone on too to drum up some excitement among the natives, some of whom might never have heard the name 'Jesus'. The deal is that Clive pays for the equipment and delivers the gospel in word and demonstration of the Spirit (1 Corinthians 2:4) whilst Mohan picks the villages, facilitates and 'prepares the way'. The whole thing is steeped in intercession and prayer.

Mohan has a powerful deliverance ministry; tormented souls flock to his humble church (it looks like a large breeze block cattle shed) from near and far to receive ministry for weeks at a time. Whilst I was there the church was crammed with twenty or thirty people camped out on the floor. Inside its sparse and gloomy interior it looked like a make shift wartime hospital – which is exactly what it was (Ephesians 6).

It appears that word gets out that 'this god Jesus' is the answer to their spiritual bondage. So people just turn up on the doorstep, get loved and prayed for daily in the name of Jesus and stay until their demons have been cast out and they are free. Then they join the church community. I met a former Hindu priestess who used to teleport in the spirit. She served me the sweetest afternoon tea and had eyes like wells of light.

Clive and Mohan have worked together for a number of years and despite an apparently insurmountable language barrier they clearly have a deep understanding and common goal. Each night we went to a different village, within the equivalent of Mohan's parish vicinity and each night between a hundred or two hundred locals would turn out to see what all the fuss was about. On one occasion I got caught up in a very amusing cricket match with some local children. They were wildly enthusiastic, unsurprisingly talented and would repeatedly shout 'Flintoff' at me through slightly inane ivory white grins. More a reference to my Anglo Saxon 'bottle', I think, than my all-round capability. Although relatively-speaking I did bowl extremely fast at them.

Clive and I took it in turns to give our testimonies and preach the gospel (at that stage in my preaching career, an entirely unmerited grace on his part) and we saw many healings and demons cast out. Each evangelistic outreach that week was wonderfully different and each merits attention but for the sake of time there is one powerful experience that I would like to leave you with.

On the first night, once Clive had preached the death and resurrection of Jesus Christ for the forgiveness of sins and salvation of the world, we went into a time of corporate ministry. We cried out for God to pour out His spirit and then Clive and I began to "lay hands on" the villagers, most of whom had come

Preaching the gospel in a village in India

up to the foot of the stage for prayer. I rather reluctantly laid hands on a girl whom I assumed was clearly already a Christian as she had arrived at the village with our party. At that stage I did not see the need for praying for Christians!

Within about a minute she slumped to the floor under the power of the Holy Spirit, her fall partly broken by the turbulent crowd. I was rather encouraged and looked around for my next 'victim'. Then to my increasing surprise she started to struggle to her feet whilst shaking her head violently and throwing her arms around recklessly. Her face was contorted and her eyes were scrunched up tightly. Whilst friends tried to control her aggressive movements she made a bee line for me and a look of cold, steely hatred came over her eyes. Her eyes had totally changed from when she had initially approached me; they were now totally dead.

For the first time I truly understood what Jesus meant when He said, "The eye is the lamp of the body. If your eyes are good, your whole body will be full of light. But if your eyes are bad, your whole body will be full of darkness. If then the light within you is darkness, how great is that darkness!" (Matthew 6 vs. 22 and 23) Then the girl started to hurl verbal abuse at me in the local dialect, Tamil. I quickly discerned a demonic presence (I had had no practical experience in this but it was glaringly obvious) and commanded the spirit to leave in the name and by the blood of Jesus. I confidently took authority over the spirit and persisted in my rebuke but the girl, or spirit within her more accurately, continued to bellow and fight with me. Eventually Clive arrived on the scene and said that I should leave her as it was causing too much of a commotion and might be frightening people. Indeed at that moment her friends carted her away.

Moments later my translator turned to me laughing and described matter-of-factly how the spirit within the girl had been repeatedly shouting, "Have you come here to cast me out also?" I later heard that this girl has been receiving deliverance for some months from many different people. It transpired that this girl had been deeply involved in Hinduism and that this evil spirit had refused to come out despite many powerfully anointed people of God praying for her. Shades of Mark chapter 9 (v 17 onwards)

'Then one of the crowd answered and said, "Teacher, I brought You my son, who has a mute spirit. And wherever it seizes him, it throws him down; he foams at the mouth, gnashes his teeth, and becomes rigid. So I spoke to Your disciples, that they should cast it out, but they could not." He answered him and said, "O faithless generation, how long shall I be with you? How long shall I bear with you?

Bring him to Me." Then they brought him to Him. And when he saw Him, immediately the spirit convulsed him, and he fell on the ground and wallowed, foaming at the mouth. So He asked his father, "How long has this been happening to him?" And he said, "From childhood. And often he has thrown him both into the fire and into the water to destroy him. But if You can do anything, have compassion on us and help us."

Jesus said to him, "If you can believe, all things are possible to him who believes." Immediately the father of the child cried out and said with tears, "Lord, I believe; help my unbelief!" When Jesus saw that the people came running together, He rebuked the unclean spirit, saying to it, "Deaf and dumb spirit, I command you, come out of him and enter him no more!" Then the spirit cried out, convulsed him greatly, and came out of him. And he became as one dead, so that many said, "He is dead." But Jesus took him by the hand and lifted him up, and he arose. And when He had come into the house, His disciples asked Him privately, "Why could we not cast it out?" So He said to them, "This kind can come out by nothing but prayer and fasting."

This stuff is second nature to these Indian believers, there was no hint of a disproportionate interest in the devil but simply an awareness of the spiritual reality and battle that supercedes the material. They live the gospel in all its love, suffering, joy and power. They are spiritual people and they care less about flesh and blood. Let us take a leaf out of their book, the Bible, and remember Paul's famous mandate, *"Put on the whole armour of God, that you may be able to stand against the wiles of the devil. For we do not wrestle against flesh and blood, but against principalities, against powers, against the rulers of the darkness of this age, against spiritual hosts of wickedness in the heavenly places. Therefore take up the whole armour of God, that you may be able to withstand in the evil day, and having done all, to stand."* (Ephesians 6:11-13)

One thing my Indian experience taught me is the sheer spiritual reality of the universe and the fact that God really is God. And that ain't changing. Whether we like it or not. You can either seek and chase after God, Jesus Christ, or you can be distracted by other gods, worse, enslaved by demons. Either way, we're all in a spiritual battle for our worship. I realised then, and God help me realise today, that I needed and wanted more of the only true God in my life.

CHAPTER 10
"FROM GLORY TO GLORY, MESSILY"

When I arrived back in Britain, I knew that the supernatural realm was just as active, the worship and idolatry just as prevalent and the British people just as lost, addicted, bound and in need of Jesus Christ as anywhere else in the world. The Great Commission is not confined to missionaries in the third world, it's a lifestyle and I had caught the bug well and truly. So in the grace and leading of the Holy Spirit, fuelled by what felt like an ever increasing God-given passion for lost souls and with the help of a group of red-hot brothers and sisters I founded a street church in the red light district of Soho, London, called Now Believe.

We purchased a second-hand truck and for seven years we met at 7pm nearly every Thursday night whatever the weather on the corner of Brewer street. We prayed, chatted with people, sang worship songs and preached the gospel openly, ministering to drug addicts, the homeless, the pimps, sex addicts, the LGBTQ community, the working girls, the rich, the cool and the famous. There is no partiality with God, Jesus is Saviour to all.

We gave out free cups of tea and coffee, homemade sandwiches and cakes, leaflets and Bibles and we prayed for the sick. I had a ten-foot wooden cross made and we erected that next to the sex shops, Chinese restaurants and brothels. Crowds would form and we saw healings and demons manifest and flee. Some people insulted and mocked us, others drunkenly hurled bottles of beer at us, the homeless hugged us, the offended reported us to the council, so many folk laughed and cried with us, and wonderfully some knelt on the grimy streets next to the ruddy cross and gave their lives to Jesus with us.

The local working girls, touts and even pimps became our friends, they would turn up eagerly each week and miss us when for whatever reason we couldn't come – truly we had church family without walls. It was a glorious season and our spiritual family consisted of all sorts of believers amassed from different denominations and different parts of the country.

Our street church in Soho, London, which ran for 7 years

Soon we purchased a stage and took this little gospel outreach to Trafalgar square and then different cities around the nation (www.roarthegospel.org). We have seen street ministry teams of over 100 believers gather to reach out to their local neighborhoods. I have had the excitement and privilege of encouraging people who have hardly ever spoken in public get up on a stage and speak out their testimony of salvation in front of perfect strangers on the streets of their city. The roar of the lion of Judah is returning to the church.

My wife Thea and I preaching the gospel
from a stage in Trafalgar square, London

Alongside my thirst to see more fruit and more power the Lord brought me into ministry school twice and intense seasons of personal healing, repentance and pruning under different ministries. When we come into the kingdom, we are born again, the old has gone and everything is new. We are the righteousness of God in Christ Jesus, completely forgiven and our old "Adamic" nature has been crucified with Christ, buried with Christ and we are raised in Him holy, blameless and without reproach. But there is an invitation to repentance, renewal of the mind, a cleansing of the soul and an apprehending of our inheritance, by faith. Old agreements and strongholds must be forsaken, new truth walked in; it's both a glorious and messy process of sanctification which the Holy Spirit leads us in graciously.

Slowly but surely God will lead us to take off every mask and counterfeit covering, even our carefully crafted religious/ministry ones that are perhaps most subtle. We have to be willing to humble ourselves and come into the light, to trust in God's goodness and love. This involves bringing our hurts, our secrets and our shame out of the shadows of graceless perfectionism ("by the law is the knowledge of sin" so legalism's demand is perfection), condemnation and self-righteousness into the light of the truth, receiving fully the righteousness of Christ in the process.

Throughout my time of pursuing more of God I have had many victories and made many mistakes, and I have come under much persecution, although not yet to the shedding of blood. Many friends and family simply couldn't handle my new faith and passion to preach the gospel. In retrospect, I realize that at times I could have acted with more wisdom, discernment and compassion.

When I was too zealous in the church, so called mature believers would try and throw water on my bonfire. Holy fire should be corralled, never dampened. At other times, I'd be difficult to lead and manage, or I would slip into self-righteous legalism or pride, doing myself and the kingdom of God no favours. I have had seasons of isolation both Spirit led and through my own hurt and rejection. I have learned that it is not what happens to us in life that really matters but how we respond. The Lord has redemption, spiritual upgrade and character formation in every season, His heart is to form Christ in His children. God rewards fruitfulness with pruning, that we might bear more fruit. Don't waste your trials nor despise the day you are in, even if its fruit seems paltry to you. The Lord knows what He is doing – just stay in faith!

Some of the lessons I have learned (and am still learning), about grace, wilderness, rest, identity, sacrifice, courage, zeal and the everlasting love of the Father, I have attempted to capture in the devotions that follow in this book. Each occasion either under a healing ministry, counseling or at ministry school (it's all the school of the Holy Spirit) has served as a powerful springboard into more fruit and more local and international short-term mission.

Preaching the gospel in Ethiopia

By the grace of God I have gone on to preach the gospel and minister in Sri Lanka, South Africa, Kenya, Brazil, Ehiopia and the US witnessing many signs, wonders and miracles. In 2009 the Lord called me to start a discipleship school called 'Growing in the Supernatural' and eventually I had the privilege of founding a three day worship festival with my friends called 'David's Tent'. This fiery gathering annually hosts thousands of worshippers in the UK and now the US, who meet to worship God and press into His presence for 72 hour periods. Praise God.

Brothers and sisters, friends, don't waste your life. Violently, passionately pursue Jesus with everything you have and don't let anything get in the way of that. Let Him into every nook and cranny of your life. Become all He intended you to be. Seek your God, know your God, manifest your God, scream your God to a lost world. We have one life, there's no dress rehearsals and very soon your soul will be required of you and you'll be standing there right in front of Him. That is love.

DEVOTIONS FROM A LIFE OF BURNING

DAY 1
THE FATTED CALF

"Your smile destroys my religion."
Jonathan Helser

It is possible to work for God and miss your entire calling and inheritance. The elder brother in the parable of the prodigal illustrates this chillingly. What a horrible thought. And what a stinking church it yields.

Many Christians get stuck in the slave mentality; unwittingly refusing what the Father has for them to receive freely. The elder brother in Luke 15 was bent on working for something that he could only inherit through intimate relationship and bloodline. Indeed "slaves" (and prodigals) find it very hard to replace their rags and toil with family rings, royal robes, sandals of sonship, dancing, partying and eating the best steak right next to Dad – without somehow *earning* it. Our shame runs deep and the accuser's voice speaks loud with religious language.

Working for a paycheck makes too much sense. So, the unworthy hit hard the fields of performance, shun the intimacy and generosity of paternity.

Even the returning prodigal was readied with a speech on "unworthiness" (Luke 15:9). It all sounds pious and humble, but it is proud and stubborn. I still regularly have to refuse this "unworthy" lyric in many contemporary worship songs that come my way in church. I am standing alongside believers who are supposed to have been thriving in the Father's house for a couple of decades. I get that we don't deserve or earn our blessing but we are *worth it* to Father – Jesus has proved that for all time.

Unworthiness is a hard task-master, a very shrewd lie, and false humility is a great temptation. As the elder brother modelled, in spite of the Father's plea to each of us (Luke 15:28,31), I am the only one who can say goodbye to unworthiness and the servants' quarters, receive my intrinsic worth, sonship, and move into the Father's house for good (John 8:35). There alone is my free and royal inheritance (1 Peter 2:9). I won't even get so much as a skinny goat out in the field and I am likely to spoil a hat full of parties along the way. May I dare to come home, allow myself to be celebrated and kissed – and then stay there.

DAY 2
HEAVEN'S IDENTITY

Religion: 'My identity is built on being a good person.'
Gospel: 'My identity is not built on my record or
my performance but on Christ's.'
Tim Keller

A Christian's root identity is in Christ. So we Christians are not sinners, we are saints, hidden in Christ. Our God is not angry with us, He's thrilled and head over heels in love (Matthew 3:17). All righteous wrath has been exhausted in the body of Christ on the cross, once, for all (Hebrews 9:12, 25-28), and He remembers our sin no more (Hebrews 8:12-13). Our future is not lack and guilt but abundant grace, His righteousness, hope, in spite of trials and persecutions, blessing and reigning in life (Romans 5:17).

Speaking the truth in love to a person is not telling them their dysfunctions but calling out their true identity. "Hey, you don't need to be doing this because this is who you *really* are." Accountability is not watching each other's sin patterns but calling each other on our gold, ensuring we "account" for our "abilities" – who heaven says we are and what heaven says we carry. We always overcome evil with good, the dark behaviour caused through lies, with the truth (light) that brings freedom.

Graham Cooke said this: *"Here's the thing about God – whenever He connects with you He does so by how He sees you in the spirit, not by how we are behaving. He's always speaking to your identity. He's always speaking to who you really are. Once God tells you your persona, once he reveals this to you this is how you are known in heaven. That's the way He speaks to you from that point on."*

The crowd saw Zacchaeus as a corrupt money-grabbing thief of Israel. They were livid when Jesus chose to have lunch with him.

But Jesus saw him at the end of his race. The grace and kindness of Jesus punctured through his hard walls of rejection and greed, leading to Zacchaeus moving in earth-shattering repentance and generosity. Once Zacchaeus had repented Jesus further called him out: *"Zacchaeus too is a [real spiritual] son of Abraham."* Heaven only knows whom Zacchaeus went on to become.

Gideon effectively called himself a powerless weed. God called him *"a mighty man of [fearless] courage"*. That's what Gideon became. Once you are born again by repentance and faith you are a new creation, a saint, a royal priest. Receive who God says you are, day after day, and watch how you slowly become it. What we agree with, we empower. That's how the spirit realm works.

Our healthy "do" always flows from our healthy "who". The power of the heavenly-minded is that our hearts and our minds are always in sync with who God is for us and who we are to Him. Every single thing in our life is relational. I will say it again, every problem, every difficulty, it's all about who God wants to be for us and who He says we are. Be a son first and then everything else will line up properly.

DAY 3
SHAM GLAM TO GLORY

*"I think everybody should get rich and famous
and do everything they ever dreamed of,
so they can see that it's not the answer."*
Jim Carrey (Hollywood Actor)

It's taken me forty years on this earth and fifteen years of walking with Jesus to realize the following. Don't ever be envious of people who are chasing after the merry go round of the world or living in sin and compromise – bound by the pride of life, the lust of the eyes, the lusts of the flesh. It's tempting to think that you are missing out on all the fun.

Friends, sin never keeps its promises – the wages are meager, only addiction, death and impending judgment. No joy, no real hope, no lasting peace, no ultimate purpose, no agape love, just a heck of a lot of self, ego, shallow pleasures, vanity, addictions, anxiety, restlessness, fear, hang overs, shame and guilt, jealousies, contentions, vapid consumption, insecure manipulations, outbursts, never feeling fulfilled, never having quite enough, never being cool enough. Piling in as much so called fun, rat-racing and quasi-meaning as you can into eighty godless, decrepit years that will (ultimately) amount to nothing – and worse.

The life of sin, the life without Jesus as Lord, Saviour and good Shepherd is a sorry, rip off life. Let's call it for what it is. There's absolutely nothing cool about being a slave to the devil. I repeat – nothing.

I feel like we need to get that clear in this very loud YouTube frenzied world of sham glamour and existential emptiness. Thank God for Jesus and the glorious Holy Spirit of the Living God within you. Wow. Now that's cool. Boast in His cross, church, glory in

His resurrection - preach His gospel loud. Yes, all humanity does need a Saviour. And yes, this message is offensive. It does rattle the walls of our death-cages. But it's offensively good news to the humble. Death and darkness has been defeated. The gospel is honestly the only thing worthy of boasting in, all else is dog turd in a plastic bag compared to the surpassing greatness of knowing Him.

Today, may you enjoy that ecstatic sparkle that only He can put in your eyes, savor the bliss that radiates from your inner man, yield to His propensity in you for kindness, goodness, gentleness, faithfulness and self-control. May you get excited by the life of miracles, the free gift of righteousness and the kingdom purpose you have as you walk with Him. Look forward to the eternal reward and unfathomable joy that is coming for you as a covenant promise. Come on! O Jesus. Point people to the beauty of holiness and may you desire more and more of Him – that's freedom, that's life in it's fullness. Seriously.

DAY 4
THE GIFT OF GRATITUDE

"To be grateful is to recognise the love of God in everything He has given us – and He has given us everything. Every breath we draw is a gift of His love, every moment of existence is a grace, for it brings with it immense graces from Him."

Thomas Merton

The gift of a grateful heart is perhaps the greatest virtue there is. Indeed, the absence of gratitude produces a terrible vacuum which must be filled. Thanklessness is actually the entrance of darkness (Romans 1:21). When our gratitude is off, our coveting is on. Envy, entitlement, greed, lust, a controlling spirit, restlessness, self-pity and depression follow in the slip stream. In our wrong focus, we are fostering a poverty spirit and incessant lack will be our portion.

In contrast, when we show gratitude, we step into abundance. The fruit of thanksgiving is a wealth mind-set – generosity, kindness, a heart to encourage, honour, graciousness, preference of others, meekness, trust and joy. Gratitude even brings supernatural multiplication. Jesus accepted the boy's packed lunch and gave thanks before doling it out to thousands.

Go hard after thankfulness. *"In everything give thanks"* (1 Thessalonians 5:18); not *for* everything, but *in* everything. Give the gift of thanks to the Giver, who in His generous, merciful giving, changes not. Everything good is from Him. Take time in the giving. Make a list perhaps, speak it out loud – savour the thank you gift you are giving, go into detail. Enter His gates of glory with this simple, hell-emptying, Spirit-filling act of thanksgiving (Psalm 100). Be set free, the grass is not greener on "the other side", it's in the watering. Your fullness of joy is not in your acquisition, it's in your appreciation and in the thick of His presence alone (Psalm 16:11).

DAY 5
ON HIS SHOULDERS

*"And when he has found it, he lays it
on his shoulders, rejoicing."*
Luke 15:5

Repentance is changing your thinking, beliefs and life-direction back to God. This allows God to transform your entire life and destiny. This is repentance: when you consent to be saved, when you consent to be loved, when you consent to be carried by His arms of strength, when you consent to be carried by the arms of His love. Repentance requires the humility to let God love you, let God "do" for you and through you. Repentance is fully apprehending grace, through intimacy.

All of us inherited a pre-disposition to living independently from God. We have been discipled by the world in feasting from the tree of the knowledge of good and evil, which might be called the tree of independence and self-righteousness. This tree kills. Indeed, self-righteousness, rooted in pride, is the mother of all sin. Remember, there are still two trees in the garden. Repentance is turning away from playing god and turning back to the true God, feeding from the tree of intimacy and dependence, the tree of life – Jesus.

But the story we're given is a God-story, not an Abraham-story. What we read in Scripture is, "Abraham entered into what God was doing for him, and that was the turning point." (Romans 4:1-3 MSG)

Repentance is not striving and wailing in false humility before the altar. Yes, there is godly sorrow – but repentance is consenting, turning round, yielding to grace. All other religions say "DO DO DO!" Jesus says: "DONE DONE DONE!"

Repentance is eyes off ourselves and onto Jesus, eyes off our story, our works and onto His finished work at Calvary. St Paul writes, *"To this end I also labour, striving according to His working which works in me mightily"* (Colossians 1:29). In other words, our striving is always accomplished in His grace and mighty power. When our boast is no longer in what we can do, but what Jesus has done, there the divine exchange is activated.

So, repentance is entering into what God wants to do for us. Bono put it like this: "Don't ask God to bless what you are doing. Find out what God is blessing and join in." Repentance is turning from legalistic, orphan-hearted exhaustion to childlike trust, grace and rest. Repentance is being carried over His shoulders like a lost sheep, found like a precious coin, run toward, embraced, kissed, clothed in the best and letting the Father bless and celebrate you. Have you entered the party that is the Father's house (Luke 15)? Or are you refusing to leave the fields of self-righteousness, legalism and quiet bitterness? You'd be amazed at how hard our unworthiness and self-righteousness dies. Let the Father love you today. Consent to being His "beloved", let him bless you as the "blessed." That's repentance – right believing, which leads to right living.

DAY 6
LEAN IN

*"The most loving thing we can do for
anyone is introduce them to Jesus."*
Billy Graham

Have you noticed how it's relatively easy to talk about God and God's love to people in the streets? It's a great place to start. It usually won't offend anyone. Although even "God" has become a bit of a taboo in some places in the west recently. But it also probably won't challenge them to live any differently either. There's no power in the word "God". All the power is in the name "Jesus".

The things you find most embarrassing (that's the self-consciousness of the flesh) to proclaim publicly usually carry the most power in the spirit. Words like Jesus, the cross, repentance, sin, the need to be "born again", eternal life in "Christ alone". These words offend the flesh because they disturb the status quo. They have power in the spirit because they lead to the salvation of a soul.

The apostle Paul wrote – "I, brethren, when I came to you, did not come with excellence of speech or of wisdom declaring to you the testimony of God. For I determined not to know anything among you except Jesus Christ and Him crucified . . . in demonstration of the Spirit and of power." (1 Corinthians 2)

Paul understood that when we share the crucified Jesus the Holy Spirit moves. Lean into following the Holy Spirit and bringing the full message of the gospel. Lean into discomfort and full dependence on God. Build muscle and infuse integrity into your evangelism. Love people where they are at, show grace, speak truth as you feel led to – and don't apologize. Jesus never apologized for upsetting people and ruining their theological grid. Jesus never went after people to preserve his reputation or keep ministry stats looking good. Only the truth, Jesus, sets people free. People don't need a whimsical New Age message about some impersonal, pic 'n' mix god that cannot save. They need the message of love, grace and salvation power through the cross and resurrection of Jesus.

There is a cost to this. It's not always comfortable and you won't always make friends in the process, in some cases far from it. But people can always discern whether you really loved them and in almost every case you will have been a truer friend than most – for true love lays its life down for another's ultimate good (John 15:13). I like to remind myself of this: if I am not running into the devil once in a while, then I am likely walking a road and talking the talk he has no problem with. So, rejoice when you are persecuted for righteousness – great shall be your reward in heaven.

Be encouraged, sometimes it is only the word or action which really slays, following which you will see no apparent fruit at the time (perhaps the very opposite), which years later will have produced a whole harvest of righteousness (John 12:24). Don't be so quick to rate your effectiveness, put your ministry and the people whom you minister to in the hands of God. Robert Louis Stevenson put it this way – "Don't judge each day by the harvest you reap but by the seeds that you plant."

DAY 7
BOLD AS LIONS

"The righteous are as bold as a lion."
Proverbs 28:1

Let me ask you a question. Are you a sinner? Or are you a saint? A bold church is full of saints. An endlessly placating, cowering and intimidated church is one who is not sure of her righteousness. Boldness comes through righteousness. Sinners might be aggressive, but the root is fear-based. If I am born again, however I feel about myself, and however you feel about me, for that matter, God sees me as beloved, perfect, as a saint. I love feeding from the lives of the saints of old. But saints aren't just dead people on stained glass windows. In truth, every saint is alive forevermore! My point is, saints are simple people who have made Jesus Lord and Saviour. Any of us. Righteousness is never worked for. It's only ever a free gift from Jesus, received by faith and with a lifetime subscription to abundance of grace. (Romans 5:17)

Jesus said, *"Woe to you when all men speak well of you . . . rather rejoice when you are persecuted for righteousness' sake"* (Luke 6:26). Tough words. None of us enjoy rejection. A church who is insecure in her love relationship with the Lord will trade that first love for the world's acceptance. In so doing, she betrays both the Lord and the very ones she is called to love in the truth. When I am utterly satisfied and secure in my place as the beloved, as righteous in God's sight, then I can love the lost in the truth and suffer persecution with Christ, counting it all joy. To live is Christ, to die is more life. The content of the sermon is not what people take away with them. People are scarred by the direction and flavour of your adoration and the God or gods you truly belong to. People can smell worship. People can tell the God or god you preach by whom you are trying to placate. Before whom does your life really stand? This generation doesn't want Ted Talk sheen, clever lighting displays and bottom-kissing relevance. They long to comprehend reverence. They want something worthy of giving their lives for. They want Almighty God.

Charles Stanley said, "His voice leads us not into timid discipleship but into bold witness." Let's throw out the falsely humble, works-based gospel and step into our place of abundant grace and our identity as the righteousness of God in Christ Jesus. If you believe you are a sinner, you will sin by faith. If you know that you, the real you, are now "holy, blameless and without reproach" (washed clean by the blood of Jesus), you'll walk in that holy, heaven-sent reality more and more. And the righteous are bold as a lion. The church is waking up to who she really is and *whose* she is. Boldness, that anointed roar, is returning.

DAY 8
THE OFFENSE OF CALVARY

"Blessed are those who are persecuted for righteousness' sake, for theirs is the kingdom of heaven. "Blessed are you when they revile and persecute you, and say all kinds of evil against you falsely for My sake. Rejoice and be exceedingly glad, for great is your reward in heaven, for so they persecuted the prophets who were before you. You are the salt of the earth; but if the salt loses its flavour, how shall it be seasoned? It is then good for nothing but to be thrown out and trampled underfoot by men."

Matthew 5:10-13

I have been in love with Jesus just over 15 years. I still vividly remember the day that I finally stopped running from God, repented of my sins and received Jesus as my Lord and Saviour. Everything changed in an instant. The Holy Spirit flooded my soul with the most glorious love, joy, peace and ecstasy. Words are utterly inadequate to describe what took place then and the loving Presence which continues to follow and fill my life to this day. I will say I knew that heaven and hell were real, that death had lost its sting, that I would spend eternity with my heavenly Father and that, well, everyone needed to know about the reality of this crucified and resurrected Jesus Christ. So, I started getting out there in the sea of humanity, going after the lost, opening my mouth and telling people about Jesus. The rest has been salty, bewildering and exciting history.

"Revival is not the discovery of some new truth. It's the rediscovery of the grand old truth of God's power in and through the Cross."

(Sammy Tippit)

In all my "going" I have discovered that the message of the cross of Christ is both the place of greatest offence among people and greatest power over darkness. Those who carry the message of the cross and resurrection of Jesus are the true 'salt of the earth' – their portion is offence or joy with man but always reward in heaven. The cross is glad tidings to the humble but offensive to the proud, both the religious and the rebellious.

For example, secular humanism is at war with the cross. At the root is the pride of man and self-righteousness. Many in the public sphere will encourage the church to feed the poor, free the sex slaves, volunteer for charities (all great "kingdom" endeavours) as long as she does not preach the gospel – sin, grace, repentance, the cross and resurrection. In many camps you can talk vaguely about God, but don't mention Jesus. Both carnal and legalistic man will never cease to be offended by the cross of Christ and will forever try to replace it with another type of sacrifice.

Rick Joyner writes,

"Since Cain and Abel, the sacrifice has been the main point of conflict between the two seeds, which represent the two natures of man – carnal and spiritual. Satan is not threatened if we embrace the doctrines of the institution of Christianity; in fact, he may well encourage it. He knows that the good of the Tree of Knowledge is just as deadly as the evil and far more deceptive. Human goodness is an affront to the cross and is used as a compensation for it. It deludes us into thinking that if we do more "good" than evil, we will be acceptable to the Father, thereby placing us above the need for the sacrifice of His Son. Satan may well encourage us to embrace anything religious as long as we do not turn to the cross."

(Extract from There Were Two Trees in the Garden)

DAY 9
THE CROSS

*"It is more urgent than at any time in history that the
church preach the plain, pure Gospel, focusing on
Jesus and the Cross, an eternal perspective, things
above, and an awareness of heaven and hell."*

Rolland Baker

When it comes to faith in Jesus there are just two types of
people; the enemies of the cross (conscious or unconscious), or
those who boast in the cross. The cross is the unapologetic line
in the sand between those who trust in their own righteousness,
however spiritual or secular that might look, or those who have
truly repented of their sin, been consciously saved and filled with
the Holy Spirit and have made Jesus Lord, trusting in His finished
work at Calvary and blood covering alone.

Only the unconditional love and grace of God the Father in
the cross of His Son Jesus deals with both the resentful, po-
faced, religious legalism of the "elder brother" and the licentious
rebellion of the "younger brother", squandering his inheritance
far from God (Luke 15). The acquitting mercy of God and the
justice of God (someone has to pay) meet at the cross. Only at
the cross was condemnation, wrath and the righteous judgment
of a Holy God exhausted, that we through faith might be forgiven,
saved, healed, delivered, justified, adopted and become the very
righteousness of God in Christ Jesus!

Only at the cross was the power of sin, death and the devil
defeated. Only by Jesus's guiltless offering at the cross was the
death-wage of our sin swallowed up in resurrection victory. At
Calvary alone, through repentance and faith, can carnal man
(in all his expressions) be slain with Christ, the Adamic body of
death be put off once and for all (in the watery grave of baptism),

so that the Spirit can live through new creation children of God, made ready for heaven and set free. Every man dead in sin and then born again to live and reign in resurrection life. That's the gospel. That's very good news.

The fake gospel in the crowd-pleasing church is fundamentally cross-less and so devoid of the resurrection power of the Holy Spirit. Going out like a decorative candle on a church altar at the end of a dry liturgy, it isn't and can't save anyone. My point is, whatever your preferred expression of worship, beautiful liturgy or electric light displays, it must centre around Jesus Christ, Him crucified and a demonstration of the Spirit (1 Cor 2:1-5) – not clever man power. The true gospel is coming to our shores that will make men and women into new creations once again, ablaze in the Spirit of God, unstoppable in their witness, unabashed in their testifying! Get ready. The cross is about to be preached in the church and the market places like never before. It will separate the wheat from the chaff, those who really just love the world and their quaint religion versus those who love Jesus the Lamb of God and Bridegroom, pining to live for His reward, second coming and Glory alone.

DAY 10
THE SPOKEN WORD
PART 1

*"Disturb the normal. In the culture you live in,
there is a subtle social normal that intimidates
people from being bold for the Gospel. It gets into
our minds somehow that by sharing Jesus we are
bothering people. We have found that there are two
types of people in this world: those who accept
where this world is at and keep quiet, or those who
choose to rebel against it because they want people
to see the power of the truth. As believers we are the
voice, the shaking and source of boldness that
God uses to change culture."*

Ben Fitzgerald

My wife Thea and I recently went dancing in Long Street, Cape Town. There's one memory that won't leave me from that night. Whilst walking the streets, every 20 metres, we were disturbed by a cocaine dealer offering us drugs. That regularly, for real. These guys have some boldness and ambition. How much more the church?

We live in a time in the West where the word "preach" has become a dirty word. The Greek word for 'preach' is "kerusso"; it means to proclaim or announce in the manner of a herald, bringing important news. This word is used over 60 times in the New Testament.

If love is the fuel of the Christian life, then preaching is the spark which lights the fire. We all preach. People who tell you not to preach are "preaching" that exact message of intolerance, ironically. All people announce the news they hold most dear, out of every heart mouths are proclaiming, to the degree that their influence and passion carries them. When it comes to Christians, sadly many have been intimidated into diluting truth or outright silence by the antichrist system of the world (in short this is the spirit which John wrote about in 1 John 4) or the overly seeker-sensitive church. Multitudes have bowed and got muzzled without even knowing it.

AW Tozer said this – "We who preach the gospel must not think of ourselves as public relations agents sent to establish good will between Christ and the world. We must not imagine ourselves commissioned to make Christ acceptable to big business, the press, the world of sports or modern education. We are not diplomats but prophets, and our message is not a compromise but an ultimatum."

Atheist Penn Jillette said this: "I've always said that I don't respect people who don't proselytise. I don't respect that at all. If you believe that there's a heaven and a hell, and people could be going to hell or not getting eternal life, and you think that it's not really worth telling them this because it would make it socially awkward – and atheists who think people shouldn't proselytise and who say just leave me alone and keep your religion to yourself – how much do you have to hate somebody to not proselytise? How much do you have to hate somebody to believe everlasting life is possible and not tell them that? I mean, if I believed, beyond the shadow of a doubt, that a truck was coming at you, and you didn't believe that truck was bearing down on you, there is a certain point where I tackle you. And this is more important than that."

Church, we have atheists knocking us into shape and calling out divine destiny. Jesus commanded it. I, for one, won't be silent about it – "Preach the gospel!" Let's get out there in the streets and deal resurrection life. Bother people. Disturb the death-sleep. Throw yourselves into the furious and broad way of destruction – stop people from being hit by the truck of idolatry, addiction and damnation.

DAY 11
THE SPOKEN WORD
PART 2

*"Nothing happens in the kingdom
without a declaration."*
Bill Johnson

"Preach the gospel" is the near number one command of Jesus when He commissioned His disciples into a lost world. Is there any news more worthy of announcing than eternal life? "If God calls you to be a missionary, don't stoop to be a King", wrote Spurgeon. Preach in the market places, on social media, in the arts, on the streets, through song, on clothes, in theatre, via business. Whichever mountain of influence you are called into, preach the gospel.

Don't be put off by any sense of inadequacy (this isn't about our own little profile) or by how others have preached poorly in the past. We need to open our mouths and make noise. And trust God with the rest. People aren't waiting for you when you go out to preach, the Holy Spirit is.

The spoken word is vital. Which is why there is such a fierce battle going on over this issue of "preaching". If God didn't open His mouth and actually say something you wouldn't be here (Genesis 1:3). The big bang happens with the big preach. We are made in God's image (Genesis 1:26). When we speak truth in love, we create worlds with our words (Hebrews 11:3).

Just as in the beginning, the Spirit of God is out there hovering over the chaotic darkness in our world waiting to land on the boldly proclaimed word of God so that His kingdom can crash in. When the church stays silent, on any issue, she has already bowed to the devil and so the kingdom of darkness thrives in that area. It's the way creation has been set up (Proverbs 18:21). What you worship is evidenced by what you proclaim publicly as well as what you refuse to mention publicly. It's what you talk about that demonstrates your altar (Luke 6:45), not which denomination you belong to, or whether you made church on Sunday.

We have the high call to run with zeal and wisdom and, like Paul, remain guiltless of the blood of men by not shunning to declare the whole counsel of God (Acts 20:26-27). Crowd-pleasing 21st-century "tolerance" is counterfeit compassion and idolatry. The altar is the fear of man. We need the fear of God back. The compassion of Jesus preaches truth boldly in love, leaning into self-sacrifice for the sake of my neighbour's salvation. No greater love has man than he lay down his reputation, comfort, even life for his friend.

"We talk of the Second Coming; half the world has never heard of the first." – Oswald J. Smith

DAY 12
DARE GREATLY
PART 1

"You make me brave."
Amanda Cook

Early on in the wildfire spread of the Way, the early apostles were infamous for making forbidden, dangerous statements publicly about Jesus. As a result, they were constantly being intimidated and threatened by the authorities to keep a lid on it about Jesus. Christian faithfulness at that time looked like spending time in and out of incarceration. Neither circumstance nor man's applause dictate our success in the eyes of heaven – it is only ever faithfulness to God, working through love.

In Acts 4, following the noisy, controversial explosion of the church at Pentecost, we find Peter holding forth under the public spotlight again: *"Nor is there salvation in any other, for there is no other name under heaven given among men by which we must be saved. Now when they saw the boldness of Peter and John, and perceived that they were uneducated and untrained men, they marvelled. And they realised that they had been with Jesus."* (vs 12,13)

The scripture reads that when they saw "the boldness" of simple men they were astonished. They realised these two men had spent time with God. In other words, evidence of our communion with God results in boldness. Fear is gone, love and faith overtake, and public announcement concerning salvation follows.

But is the fruit of intimacy that simple?

The apostle Paul writes this: *"For if I preach the gospel, I have nothing to boast of, for necessity is laid upon me . . . the love of Christ compels me."* (1 Corinthians 9:16, 2 Corinthians 5:14)

Intimacy with Jesus laid necessity on Paul, divine love compelled him to preach Christ crucified.

I can relate to the experience of Peter and Paul. I am an ordinary, simple, relatively untrained lover of Jesus compelled by His love, zeal and jealousy to the streets – the perishing sea of humanity. I fear stuff. I fear rejection at times. I fear failure. One of my biggest fears is misrepresenting Him but I fear not representing Him the most. Someone said that courage isn't the absence of fear but the mastering of fear for a higher purpose. My intimacy with Jesus swallows me up in His higher purpose, His Holy Spirit makes me bold – necessity is laid upon me.

Whichever Spirit or spirits you hang out with will overtake your ambition and govern your tongue (Luke 6:45). For those concerned about misrepresenting God, there is something so powerful that Jesus encourages us with in Luke 10:16: *"He who hears you hears Me, he who rejects you rejects Me, and he who rejects Me rejects Him who sent Me."*

Step back from that word for a second. Marvel at and be deeply encouraged by the ardent loyalty of our Saviour. Tim Keller said this: "If I have the smile of God, all other frowns are inconsequential."

DAY 13
DARE GREATLY
PART 2

"Believers, look up – take courage.
The angels are nearer than you think."
Billy Graham

We stand up for Jesus with our little packed lunch of fish and bread and Jesus comes in over the top of us with the tidal wave of His Holy Spirit (John 16:8). Church, don't be afraid to stand up and preach the gospel in all your theological inadequacy, wounded heart and when your love isn't yet perfected. Whilst I want to encourage us all to grow in our knowledge of the scripture and get healed up in our hearts as much as we can, we are His ambassadors just as we are, we have the endorsement of heaven through our childlike obedience, not the quality of our execution.

Look at Ravenhill's comments on the great Baxter of Kidderminster:

"Baxter was opposed to the idea that in order to minister in the things of God a man must have the ordination of the bishops and pass through the schools of learning. He declared that he feared no man's displeasure nor hoped for any man's preferment. The latter phrase he proved by refusing a bishop's miter."

Let us now glimpse Baxter as a preacher, revivalist, and soul-winner. No gladiator ever watched the eye of a Caesar or yearned for the plaudits of men for his skill as much as this tireless Puritan looked into the face of his God in prayer and listened for the sweet voice of the Spirit. No miser ever loved his gold as Baxter loved souls. No man, trapped by human love, ever wooed a maid as this man pled with impenitent sinners. His couplet was true:

"I preached as never sure to preach again,
And as a dying man to dying men."

What would it look like if every day we ministered to the lost as though we would never get another chance before the judgment seat of Christ?

I like how Teddy Roosevelt puts it:

"It is not the critic who counts; not the man who points out how the strong man stumbles, or where the doer of deeds could have done them better. The credit belongs to the man who is actually in the arena, whose face is marred by dust and sweat and blood; who strives valiantly; who errs, who comes short again and again, because there is no effort without error and shortcoming; but who does actually strive to do the deeds; who knows great enthusiasms, the great devotions; who spends himself in a worthy cause; who at the best knows in the end the triumph of high achievement, and who at the worst, if he fails, at least fails while daring greatly, so that his place shall never be with those cold and timid souls who neither know victory nor defeat."

Today, millions of eternities are at stake. Dare greatly. Those who succeed most, fail most. In any case, love never fails. Be filled with the Holy Spirit and speak the truth even though your voice shakes. Heaven is roaring you on like a thousand Wembley Stadiums.

DAY 14
PRAY AND EXPECT

"If you believe in prayer at all, expect God
to hear you. If you do not expect, you will
not have. God will not hear you unless you
believe He will hear you; but if you believe
He will, He will be as good as your faith."

Charles Spurgeon

How we deal with disappointment is key. In those moments we have a crucial choice. Either we stand on the rock of truth, or become a victim to the violent winds and waves of lies. Disappointment is a hope deferred, which needn't make the heart sick if we are active in taking thoughts captive to truth. Otherwise the passivity of defeatism will usher in the subtle sickness of heart through unbelief, then cynicism buds, then bitterness and eventually depression, even suicide.

One way of telling how your faith walk is going is to look at your levels of expectation. Expectation is abiding faith. Hope is the expectation of good things coming and arises by the power of the Holy Spirit as we believe truth and abide there (Romans 15:13). Your hope levels tell me whether you are believing truth or lies. And your level of expectation tells me your level of abiding faith or deceived victimization. Don't just pray. Pray and expect. Raise your levels of expectation. Hear the word of the Lord – faith comes by the hearing.

DAY 15
KNOW YOUR BIBLE
PART 1

*"An unbelieved truth can hurt a man much more
than a lie. It takes great courage to back truth
unacceptable to our times. There's punishment
for it, and it's usually crucifixion."*

John Steinbeck, East of Eden (1952)

*"Never be afraid of the world's censure, its praise is much
more to be dreaded"*, warned Charles Spurgeon. This fresh
"biggot-hating" culture all over the media, largely pushed by
the antichrist, totalitarian regime of the secular left, has almost
made Bible-believing a sin, even in some churches. Not a bad
effort, I must say! In some churches we are quicker to label a
Bible-believer a Pharisee, rather than a saint. Can you discern
the times, church?

Don't tell me you love Jesus when you don't love His book.
Relevance is counterfeit holiness. It has been made an idol in
large parts of our increasingly fearful, unbelieving (and spiritually
proud) western church. We are only ever relevant when we
are holy, set apart and thus able to deliver a lost person out of
darkness and into His glorious light.

We are called to be a hothouse of salvation, healing and
deliverance, jam-packed full of radical planet-shakers desperate
for more quality meat from the pulpit, fire from heaven, half-
nights of prayer and mass excursions to the perishing streets. We
must face facts: large parts of the wider western church are
anaemic, flimsy and asleep. I am not against technology, nor
decent coffee, may all things good serve the mandate of heaven.
However, I am against the flaccid, seeker-sensitive church model
that has beguiled, muzzled and shackled a cowardly church,

seduced the Bride away from first-love freedom and destroyed her trust in the power of boldly proclaiming the simple gospel alone to save humanity.

I realise these are strong words. What I am not saying is that there aren't truly awesome things happening in the kingdom right now. But I am unapologetically calling out mixture, compromise and calling us higher for such a time as this. Deep darkness is covering the earth. It is time for His Body to arise and shine like never before. Where are the heroic Stephens, proclaiming an uncut gospel in front of their truth-hating executioners? Where are the Peters and Pauls, the Latimers and Ridleys of our day? Where is our jealousy and zeal for His name? Is our God holy or not?

A popular one these days is: "It's not the Father, Son and Holy Bible." Well, it's not far off. If you love the Holy Spirit, you'll honour His extensive letter to us. The Bible is God's word, utterly inspired by the Spirit of God. Granted, you can know the Bible without knowing God but you cannot know God without knowing the Bible. Disagreement with the word of God is agreement with a lie and when you believe a lie you empower the liar. The devil's primary motivation from the foundation of the earth has been to make us doubt God's word. "Did God really say ... ?" (Genesis 3:1 NLT) His cunning and wickedness hasn't changed. And neither has God's word, nor will it ever. (Malachi 3:6, Matthew 5:18)

DAY 16
KNOW YOUR BIBLE
PART 2

"Visit many good books, but live in the Bible".
Charles Spurgeon

The primary functions of governmental authority are empowerment and protection. The church needs to throw away all carnal, man-made church programmes and pick up the sword of the Spirit, which is the word of God. If you want the power of the Spirit you must brandish the word of God. So empowering the saints comes through faithful bible teaching (2 Tim 3:16). The church also needs to learn to call out heresy again for the glory of God's name, for the protection of the flock and the removal of false prophets (Matthew 7:15).

Sacrificing the absolute truths of God on the altars of human reasoning and political correctness is grave sin, demonic in nature (1 Timothy 4:1, Matthew 4:9-10, 2 Timothy 4:4) and very foolish and destructive (John 10:10). You make yourself the devil's pawn (he is the Father of lies) and build your house on the sand. When storms and trouble come, you are going down.

Build your house on the rock. Be sanctified by the truth, which is the word of God, work out your salvation with fear and trembling. Make sure you aren't being cooked to death slowly. Get out of the pot of boiling frogs, fast. The church in this nation needs to repent and cry out for a fresh love and holy reverence for the infallible word of Almighty God.

"But on this one I will look:
On him who is poor and of contrite spirit,
And who trembles at My word."

(Isaiah 66:2)

John Wesley said, "Put fire in your sermons or put your sermons in the fire." I'm afraid large parts of the church have traded the fire of the Spirit for the cool of the world. So strong is the tide of rebellion against God in our secular age, I have realized that if I haven't been hated on as a biggot in a few weeks then it's a mark that I'm probably backsliding, disobeying God and looking to man to meet my love-deficit. But, as a mark of my adoration and worship of its Author and my heaven-bent refusal of deception and destruction, I adore the Bible. I am a Bible-loving, Bible-believing, devil-bashing, hell-emptying, truth-heralding, freedom-bringing, scripture junkie – by the grace of God.

Right now, I believe that God is shaking both the heavens and the earth with purpose. In the next season I believe that the shaking and sifting in the earth will separate the wheat from the tares, the heavenly from the man-made. So that those *things which cannot be shaken may remain"* (Hebrews 12:25-29). May the mercy of God forbid it, but there will be those tragically led away by the harlot church into deception, spiritual adultery and slavery to sin. But I believe the Bride of Christ will humble herself, seek the face of God and, where needed, repent with godly sorrow of all pride, unbelief and cowardice regarding the handling of the word of God. Once tested, we shall come forth as a burning and shining lamp like never before. I believe that this company of believers are going to see a move of God's Spirit in the church and the nations the like of which has never been seen in all of church history. May it be so.

DAY 17
THE COMMAND TO PREACH THE GOSPEL

"You have one business on earth – to save souls."
John Wesley

Jesus commands His church to "preach the gospel" and to preach "the kingdom at hand" (Mark 16:15, Matthew 10:7). This message comes via proclaiming the cross – a heady cocktail considering the increasingly self-determining, individualist, relativist, secular-fundamentalist climate in which great swathes of the West now live. But the advancing church is a gospel-proclaiming one nonetheless (be encouraged: everyone is proclaiming something), one that disturbs the so-called peace of carnal, self-satisfied man in order to point him to the true God and redeemer and bring about the activity of the Spirit to save, heal and deliver (1 Corinthians 2:1-5).

Remember, no man has lasting peace apart from peace with God, which comes via the apparent "peace-disturbing" gospel alone (Romans 1:16). Read the book of Acts; it's less of a picnic, more a series of riots, beatings, prison sentences, mass-conversions, miracles and revivals. Jesus Himself paradoxically warned that He did not come to bring peace but division, for the sake of the only true peace that is found when we are made ready for Judgment Day (Luke 12:51-53).

So, if we are not quick to simply trust and obey God's call to go out into the world and preach the gospel, if we are easily intimidated by the offence of man, crave the praise of man, then the 'Great Commission' can easily become the 'Great Suggestion'; whilst the world goes to hell on our watch. We must keep our eyes on the prize. Eternity must be stamped on our eyeballs.

DAY 18
THEY ACT

*'And when they had called for the apostles and
beaten them, they commanded that they should
not speak in the name of Jesus, and let them go.
So they departed from the presence of the council,
rejoicing that they were counted worthy to suffer
shame for His name. And daily in the temple, and
in every house, they did not cease teaching
and preaching Jesus as the Christ.'*

Luke, Acts 5:40-42

The apostles get beaten for preaching. They rejoice in that privilege . . . and shame. So then they go preaching Christ again immediately. Not only that, mark verse 42: 'They did not cease.'

This ruins me. According to the Bible, this is normal Christianity.

The book of Acts tells the story of the early church, the first Christians. Allow me to tease you, possibly offend you. The following might be in the trailer to the movie for the book of Acts: Tongues of fire, a mighty rushing wind, strange new heavenly languages, outrageously bold preaching by simple men, deadly persecutors turned (temporarily) blind by Jesus and sovereignly made apostles without asking, sovereign Holy Spirit outpourings, eight years bedridden Paralysis healed, dead men raised, translations in the spirit, angelic visitations, stoning, mocking and heroic martyrdoms, doctrinal fights, beautiful community, angels freeing people from prison, trances, visions, lying Christians dropping dead on the spot (by the Holy Spirit), occult troublemakers being cursed with blindness by the Holy Spirit, an evil king being struck dead by an angel for lack of humility and earthquakes in prisons (during prison worship services).

God builds His church whatever man tries to do to stop it. And it's never boring. But are the above what spring to mind when you think of Christianity?

You see, there's no church building or church service in the Book of Acts – just action, celebration, persecution and revolution. Those disciples turned the world upside down then met for a burger to tell stories, comb the scripture, pray and get more bold.

When the action is over we like to build a church building and sit in it. Institution thrives where action is dormant, powerless ritual gathers around disobedience. (And we "pastors" need to make our goal unemployment). God bless every wineskin out there as long as it doesn't thwart the new wine. Because we were all born for more and heaven invades earth when His people are on fire.

We, the church, are all too prone to wave our little candle in a brightly lit studio, where Bibles are on every cushioned chair and there's inexpensive lattes next to the bookshop at the back. There you can purchase books about preaching the gospel and then read them quietly in the comfortable sofas.

How about we go to a dark place near us and just preach the gospel? It will be like a bomb went off in the spirit – as the supernatural white light of the anointing blinds, confuses and dazzles the demonic realm whilst frightening angels pour in on the ladder of our agreement, demolishing strongholds. Fear, poverty, depression and infirmity will be cast out as we walk in the love and power of God, taking back the devil-ravaged land. Dead souls revived, hell plundered, heaven populated. That seems like a good day to me.

DAY 19
MIRACLES ARE MANDATORY
PART 1

"If signs, wonders and miracles don't
happen in your church, don't call it
a church. It would be misleading."

Bill Johnson

When Jesus commissioned His disciples He said this: *"As you go, preach, saying, 'The kingdom of heaven is at hand.' Heal the sick, cleanse the lepers, raise the dead, cast out demons. Freely you have received, freely give."* (Matthew 10:7-8)

The writer of Hebrews makes a further very important point: *"How shall we escape if we neglect so great a salvation, which at the first began to be spoken by the Lord, and was confirmed to us by those who heard Him, God also bearing witness both with signs and wonders, with various miracles, and gifts of the Holy Spirit, according to His own will?"* (Hebrews 2:3-4). God approves the gospel with His own signature. What's His signature of endorsement, how does God bear witness to the preaching of the gospel? Signs, wonders, various miracles and gifts of the Holy Spirit to do His will.

Miracles have become mandatory to our witness. They are easy, because God is with us. He wants to endorse the message. We must remember that love and compassion is the means to miraculous power and love is the point of miraculous power. Miracles must point to the grace, goodness and love of God. Or we missed it.

But you were born to see impossibilities bow to the name Jesus! Because you are made in the image of God. When so-called impossibilities are interfering with righteousness, we are to remember that love has made a way through the cross and resurrection of Jesus Christ. The Holy Spirit wants to work in us and through us and confirm His gospel with accompanying signs (Mark 16).

In this place of radical faith, we are most alive. Miracles are the scrapbook of Paradise lost; this appetite for the impossible at the core of our spiritual DNA. Indeed, God is the only One who can demand fruit of the impossible because central to His call is that we walk *with* Him, the all-powerful One. There is no natural and supernatural with God, there is just natural. As Bill Johnson said, *"You know your mind is renewed when the impossible becomes logical."*

Without God we can do nothing, with God we can do everything. That's the true posture of humility. Pride, the often subconscious but perpetual focusing on our own incapability rather than God's ability, actually thwarts the miracle workings of God in and through your life.

In his epistle Peter writes an extraordinary sentence: "By his stripes we were healed." Not "are" healed, w*ere.* It is done! Arguably the most pertinent words Jesus ever spoke were from the cross, when moments after He was forsaken by God (a seeming cosmic impossibility) and moments before He gave up His spirit (an equally unsearchable mystery), He cried "it is finished." The truth is our forgiveness, redemption, healing and deliverance from every sickness in this cursed earth was purchased through Jesus' shed blood at Calvary, two thousand years ago. The question is only whether we will believe it and so go out and pick up what was paid for. And that takes faith - aggressive, rebellious, bold, immovable faith.

DAY 20
MIRACLES ARE MANDATORY
PART 2

*"There is a fruit of the Spirit that must accompany
the gift of healing and that is long-suffering."*
Smith Wigglesworth

I believe the rational, secular world needs to see this raw, miraculous power of God like never before. Much of the west is filled with unbelief, blind drunk on the pomp of the man-made. Faith is the evidence of things unseen yet in today's world the mantra is "seeing is believing." The life of faith is mocked; suffocated by orphan-hearted independence, idolatry and deception. We urgently need signs that will make us wonder again, miracles that will free us to be children again.

Todd White prayed for 800 people before he saw a single healing. John Wimber prayed for people for a year and no one was healed – people even died! John said, *"God commands it, we'll do it – irrespective of the results."* After a year the healing movement started to break out and touch the ends of the earth. Heidi Baker received a prophetic word from Randy Clark at Toronto that she would see blind eyes open. It wasn't until a year later that three blind people were then healed in one day. Figures now suggest that as many as 10,000 churches have been planted in Mozambique alone through her and her husband Rolland's ministry.

It is tempting to get fat on "church growth models" that do not require the finger of God. The church can become puffed up on the arm of the flesh, persuasive words and worldly models without even knowing it. We long to remain relevant without remembering that our relevance lies in our divine capability and not our ability to "fit in."

It takes obedience, perseverance and humility to take on the healing and miracle-working ministry that Jesus commanded, which will certainly fail unless God turns up. But He will, for He is faithful and ready *"to perform His word"* (Jeremiah 1:12). Throughout biblical history, miraculous signs have been the signature of God, the sign of his unending love and salvation.

We owe the world a revelation of the true God. Healing is a self-revelation of God's character: "I am the LORD who heals you." Let us represent His loving nature fully to a suffering world. Let powerlessness become inexcusable. There is no sickness in heaven and very little allowed in the gospels. In effect, whatever does not exist in heaven should not exist here (Matthew 6:10). Pastor Surpresa Sithole, a man who has witnessed several resurrections from the dead, said this: *"If you wait for miracles to take place, the miracles will only wait for you to move. But if you go, they will follow you. Signs and wonders are behind your back, pushing you forward so that you will experience breakthrough. Don't wait for the world to bring dead people into the church. Instead, the church has to go where dead people are. All of this is waiting for you."*

DAY 21
FRIENDSHIP

*"A rule I have had for years is: to treat the Lord
Jesus Christ as a personal friend. His is not a creed,
a mere doctrine, but it is He Himself we have."*

D.L. Moody

Jesus was and is a good friend. Jesus demonstrates the friendship, the nearness of Almighty God. If the incarnation teaches us anything, it is that God doesn't just love us or put up with us, because His divine nature requires that He must, but that He really likes us. Do you know that God likes you and wants to spend time with you? In the life of Jesus we see that God *cares* about our bodies and wants us physically well and spiritually free. We are all designed to belong and the incarnation shows us "the belonging" of God.

In the life of Christ we see that God likes hanging out with people – eating, drinking, celebrating, talking, journeying. Religious people called Jesus a greedy drunkard. He probably relaxed and laughed too much for them! The intimacy was too intense. That intimacy ("into-me-you-see") led people, leads people, to repentance. God clearly likes partying with friends and family (Luke 15:23-24), He doesn't confine 'with-ness' to ninety minutes of once-weekly, joy-quenching, bottom-clenching, pattern. A lifestyle of supernatural redemption, divine romance and consecration, celebration *and* partying is where His church is going.

DAY 22
LISTENING WITHOUT ENEMIES

"There is a difference between listening
and waiting for your turn to speak."
Simon Sinek

True listening is deeply intimate. Listening allows someone to be seen, heard and loved. Listening is attention. Attention is love. Love listens restfully. Love is comfortable in disagreement, stays home, stays present, amidst chaos. Love listens in order to understand, to hear what lies behind the words, fear hardly listens . . . and only to reply, conquer or defend.

Love has nothing to prove, fear has shame to cover. Only the truly humble cannot be humiliated or offended, because their egos refuse to respond- they were crucified with Christ at Calvary and their shame has been covered by His Royal Robe. Perfect love casts out fear and swallows up pride. Perfect love reminds me who my real enemies are. I only have three enemies: the (spirit of) the world, the flesh and the devil. Sometimes I forget who I am and whose I am; the same for the person in front of me, whom I have blindly made my enemy.

Father, help me remember my sonship. Help me see sons in orphans. Help me know just how loved I am, how ultimately safe I am, my blamelessness and righteousness in You, so that I can love others more deeply, listen more intently, and empathise with compassion, without compromising truth.

DAY 23
THY TONGUE IS THY GLORY

"Out of the abundance of the heart,
the mouth speaks."
Matthew 12:34

Notwithstanding the profound, worshipful demonstration of our actions, our tongues paint the truest picture of the altar at which we worship. In other words, if a discerning artist followed you around today and painted a canvas of your conversation, not necessarily the content but the fragrance of the incense behind what you spoke about, that picture would reveal your true god or God, not your religious affiliation, or your library of spiritual text books.

James said, *"If anyone does not stumble in word, he is a perfect man."* (James 3:2) That is a profound statement. Indeed, "Thy tongue is thy glory." Every man and woman has been given a tongue for the express use of giving glory to God. All else is a misuse. Which is why taking the Lord's name in vain (a far more profound command than what most of us understand as blaspheme) comes third in the ten commandments.

Silence, or being slow to speak and quick to listen can be a wonderful demonstration of self-control, a bridled tongue and spiritual worship towards God. Likewise, it is well worth remembering that when we are embarrassed by the word of God, when we are silent about the gospel out of fear of offense, we are loud in our idolatry. We effectively blast heaven with our exaltation of lesser gods who cannot save. His word shall not return void although silence through cowardice shall always return void. Let's give the angelic realm something to land on.

Be filled with the Holy Spirit today. What you are filled with is what you will overflow with. Like Isaiah, who lived amidst a people of unclean lips, let's ask for a live coal from the altar today, in order to speak the statutes of God purely and boldly. May we renounce all vain babble in our "unruly member" today. Let's yield our tongues ("the fire" in our mouths) to the glorious unction of the Holy Spirit. Give over our conversation to the spirit of prophecy – giving glory to God, rightly deserved, everywhere we go.

DAY 24
THE JOY OF INTEGRITY

"I am not bound to win, but I am bound to
be true. I am not bound to succeed, but I
am bound to live up to what light I have."
Abraham Lincoln

One of the truest signs of maturity, character and Christ-likeness is a person who is true to their word. If God's word failed the universe would implode (Hebrews 1:3). Right now, God's word is causing you to be. We love God, our neighbour and ourselves when we become like Him in integrity. For trust cannot resist integrity. When our lives are integrated, true, God will trust us with more power. Amidst a restless consumer culture, where feelings reign and the grass is ever greener next door, let your "yes" be "yes" and your "no" be "no". That's freedom, that's holiness.

DAY 25
THE BAIT OF SATAN

"It is impossible that no offenses should come . . .
Blessed is he who is not offended because of Me."
Jesus (Luke 17:1, Matthew 11:6)

Offence is the bait of Satan. Why? Satan knows that offense is rooted in pride. If he can snare me in pride then I am outside the grace of God. And that's a disaster. The Greek word for offend (in Luke 17:1) is 'skandalon', a word which originally referred to the part of a trap where the bait is attached. Satan wants me trapped. Satan wants me offended at God, offended at people, offended at myself. The enemy of offense is thanksgiving, rooted in humility, for all men, in all circumstances (1 Timothy 2:1-2, 1 Thessalonians 5:18).

If I can't give thanks to God for the person (any person), not necessarily their behaviour, then I am falling into offence and pride, God will be opposed to me. I have excluded myself from His grace. This is very serious. There are two pairs of shoes on offer: the shoes of thanksgiving, where God goes with me or the shoes of the accuser, where I will find myself warring against God Himself.

John Bevere (*The Bait Of Satan: Living Free from the Deadly Trap of Offense*) writes, *"Trials in this life will expose what is in your heart – whether the offense is toward God or others. Tests either make you bitter toward God and your peers or stronger. If you pass the test, your roots will shoot down deeper, stabilising you and your future. If you fail, you become offended, which can lead to defilement with bitterness. Offended people still may experience miracles, words of utterance, strong preaching, and healing in their lives. But these are gifts of the Spirit, not fruits.*

We will be judged according to fruit, not gifting. A gift is given. Fruit is cultivated."

Guard your heart as though your life depends on it. It does. Never leave something (a church, group, relationship) in offence. Always move from inward peace. Otherwise you are setting yourself up for the same thing to repeat. Bless your enemies. Bless those who revile you. Bless and thank God for those who abandon you, let you down. Bless those who are promoted ahead of you. Entrust it all into the sovereign, redemptive hands of God. All of the above is evidence that you have truly forgiven, just as He forgives you. This kind of integrity is like a walled city and if you put it into practice impregnable peace is your portion.

WHAT YOU TOLERATE DOMINATES
PART 1

*"Tolerance is the virtue of people
who do not believe in anything."*

G.K. Chesterton

Love is long-suffering and kind. However, there's a subtle but vital difference between having tolerance for a person and tolerance for sin. As followers of Jesus we are called to be patient, gracious, merciful, tolerant with people (particularly the lost), but to hate evil. This is biblical love. We must love the one made in God's image, hate the thing that destroys God's image in them and us.

The devil has cooked up a counterfeit "tolerance" recently; a tolerance of any number of wicked behaviors, and the world has made this vehicle a virtue, even a god. The enemy always comes as 'an angel of light' (2 Corinthians 11:14), to seduce God's people with convincing lies, so this should come as little surprise. Tragically, as a result millions are being led into slavery to harmful addictions and sinful, destructive behaviors in the name of love, tolerance and freedom.

John Wesley said, "What one generation tolerates, the next generation will embrace." Be under no illusion, the devil has a plan. So does Jesus, our redeemer, Amen! To be deemed 'intolerant' in today's secular west comes with a black mark and a bad-smelling stigma. "Intolerant" people are outcasts. "Bigots" are suddenly everywhere, particularly if they carry a Bible faithfully. The secular fundamentalists, under the self-induced spell of political correctness (the spiritual vacuum put in place by God will take the 'fear of God' or the 'fear of man'; we can't have neither) and caught in the web of sanctified hedonism ("If it feels right it must be right") dictate that you may be almost anything, accept, 'intolerant'. What tragic irony and hypocrisy.

Indeed, postmodern relativism struggles to call anything evil except perhaps Christians who choose to obey God in hating evil (Amos 5:15). When truth, Jesus, is thrown out, truth, the word of God, understandably becomes the enemy to those bound by another voice. I am reminded of Isaiah's chilling warning: *"Woe to those who call evil good, and good evil; Who put darkness for light, and light for darkness; Who put bitter for sweet, and sweet for bitter!"* (Isaiah 5:20) Or Paul: *"But you need to be aware that in the final days the culture of society will become extremely fierce and difficult for the people of God."* (2 Timothy 3:1 TPT).

It's a time for the church's roots to go down deep, to rejoice in the persecution that is on the rise, to know that our battle is not with people but spiritual wickedness and to love people courageously out of their bondage, full of grace and truth.

DAY 27
WHAT YOU TOLERATE DOMINATES
PART 2

*"Tolerance is a cheap, low-grade parody of love.
Tolerance is not a great virtue to aspire to.
Love is much tougher and harder."*

N.T. Wright

The apostle Paul writes that the sin we tolerate in the church, "leavens" the whole lump. Have you ever made bread? Only a little yeast is required and the whole batch is done. *"Expel the immoral",* unrepentant brother, *"don't even have lunch with him."* (1 Corinthians 5:13). The key words here are 'unrepentant' and 'brother'. Paul is not talking about friendship with unbelievers but with so-called Christians, practicing and making an unrepentant habit of sin. God is opposed to the proud. However, there is always grace for the humble, those who want to turn from their sin and receive healing.

Paul's command to "expel" offends our inclusive, globalist, morally relativist mind-sets. The gospel is inclusive in so far as everyone is welcome to come into the kingdom of God but exclusive in so far as we must come in by God's way (repentance and faith in the finished work of the cross) and carry on in His ways (by abiding in the truth). In Paul's teaching, there is not an ounce of tolerance for wolves in sheep's clothing set on devouring the sheep. We are to love all people but operate in discernment and hate evil, for we have an adversary who wants the church and the human race deceived and damned (John 10:10).

Do not be deceived, saints. Counterfeit grace, in the guise of 'tolerance' (today's western idol, preferred means of self-righteousness and Jezebel's favourite means of accusing the Ahab church) is eating some Christians alive and destroying parts of the western church. We need to pick up the sword of the Spirit, which is the word of God and cut down these lies and strongholds. We must return to the true gospel. No more sin-tolerance and devil-dominance! May we hate evil and have dominion over sin as we come under grace and live from the resurrection power within us. The gracious freedom and joy of purity and holiness is going to flood the end-time Bride of Christ.

DAY 28
GRACE DOMINATES SIN

*"For sin shall not have dominion over you, for you
are not under law but under grace."*
Paul (Romans 6:14)

The sin we tolerate, dominates. What you tolerate in your life, you have bowed in slavery to, and it has (your) permission to master you. It's like trying to serve two masters – it's impossible (Matthew 6:24). By appeasing and loving one, you will hate the other. What you love will always tell me what you hate. You cannot serve God and tolerate sin.

At the beginning of creation Cain was warned by God: *"Sin lies at the door. And its desire is for you, but you should rule over it."* (Genesis 4:7) God warned Cain of his ability to rule and reign over his carnal lust or to tolerate it and so be dominated. In other words, become a victim through surrender (wrong believing – sin never keeps its promises) or rule and reign over sin by grace, through right believing.

> *"Sharing in his death by our baptism means that we were co-buried and entombed with him, so that when the Father's glory raised Christ from the dead, we were also raised with him. We have been co-resurrected with him so that we could be empowered to walk in the freshness of new life."*
>
> (Romans 6:5 TPT)

Trying harder to live holy won't help. Neither will guilt and condemnation. Apart from the abundant grace of Jesus and the free gift of righteousness, sin has dominion over each of us. We are powerless slaves. We cannot change our behavior. As Paul writes in Romans 6:5 above, the first thing we need to do is kill off sinful Adam in each of us by dying with Christ on the cross – that's baptism. Then, "we are raised with Him" and "empowered" in Him!

This is the nub of the gospel – supernatural grace that empowers victory in our yielded, everyday lives. The gospel of grace frees us to choose the Master that will run our lives. By choosing to yield and let Jesus' resurrection life live through us, we are empowered to live right and live in victory. As we change our minds and Master (repentance) we allow *God* to transform our behavior *from the inside, out.* As we receive the free gift of righteousness we will live righteous. Today, receive the cloak of righteousness, step into the unforced and abundant rhythms of grace and have victory over sin, ruling and reigning in abundant life (Romans 5:17), through Christ Jesus.

DAY 29
RADICALISATION REDEEMED

"The greatest danger the world faces is not radical Islam, but lukewarm Christianity."
Daniel Kolenda

Radicalisation is not a dirty word, indifference is. The opposite of love is not hate, it's indifference. Radicalisation (Latin "radix" – at the root, orthodox, integrated) is entirely contextual. To be radical actually demonstrates purity and authenticity. The key issue is *what* are you radical about?

Satan perverts and twists words with good reason. Through counterfeit radical expression (mainly religious) and antichrist PR (godless, controlling media), the devil wants to take the fight out of the church, wants her in hiding and bowed to his lying seductions, held captive and blind to a counterfeit "tolerance" of all things which kill, steal and destroy the children of God. Satan wants you awash in bland, insipid, worldly uniformity. Asleep, inoffensive, no good to anyone. The truth is we either live a radical life or a watered down, compromised one.

The great missionary C.T. Studd said this: *"God's real people have always been called fanatics."*

The Lord says, "Arise and shine, be courageous, hot, zealous (radical), proclaim the good news of my cross and resurrection!" For I will never leave you! Be a radical lover, be a radical truth-teller, be radically dependent on grace, be a radical worshipper of Jesus Christ.

DAY 30
TOUGH LOVE
PART 1

"What has the church gained if it is popular but there is no conviction, no repentance, no power?"

A.W. Tozer

Love is not fickle. Truth does not bend to trend. Love is not slave to man's feelings, appetites, cravings and offense. Love is not complicit silence in the face of fear. Love is not entrenched in the latest box-set, mesmerised by the ease and technology of my home entertainment unit at the expense of following Jesus or "snatching souls from the fire" (Jude 1:23).

Love is first and foremost biblical, self-less, sacrificial, defined by God and modelled by Jesus. Love gets down and dirty in the trenches of human despair. Love acts, love speaks up bravely, love shuns cowardice and self, love is patient and kind and yet love warns. Love, like Jesus, says "you are going to hell over my dead body."

Neither is grace weak, licentious or humanistic.

Listen to the Apostle Paul –

"Herald and preach the Word! Keep your sense of urgency [stand by, be at hand and ready], whether the opportunity seems to be favourable or unfavourable. [Whether it is convenient or inconvenient, whether it is welcome or unwelcome, you as preacher of the Word are to show people in what way their lives are wrong.] And convince them, rebuking and correcting, warning and urging and encouraging them, being unflagging and inexhaustible in patience and teaching. For the time is coming when [people] will not tolerate (endure) sound and wholesome

*instruction, but, having ears itching [for something pleasing
and gratifying], they will gather to themselves one teacher
after another to a considerable number, chosen to satisfy
their own liking and to foster the errors they hold, And will
turn aside from hearing the truth."*

2 Timothy 4 (AMPC)

Here we find Paul the Apostle exhorting Timothy, his spiritual
son, in how and when to love and win the lost and how and
when to correct the erring church. We can see that it's a tough
love, a bold love, certainly when compared to how many people
in the 21st century might define "love".

Paul's gospel is the original gospel of grace but see how he
confronts the error that was going to creep in. Grace which
doesn't empower righteousness is perversion. Grace and truth
is a person, Jesus. Grace will say in one breath "Neither do I
condemn you . . ." and in the next "Go and sin no more", with the
spiritual power readily available in the words to fulfil the task.

There is a very deceptive, cheap grace offered up right now
by the man-fearing, politically-correct church. So-called leaders
high up in church corridors are compromising and sacrificing
the absolute truths of God on the altars of human relevance
and political acceptability. In doing so they are shutting up the
kingdom to those who might otherwise have entered in under
the conviction of the word of God and putting countless souls in
danger of eternal separation with their watered-down, gospel
of idolatry.

These are wolves dressed cleverly as sheep. Consequently,
they cannot truly love the sheep; they are either deceived,
loving themselves and their ecclesiastical careers, both or worse.
Self-monikered ambassadors of the church of Jesus Christ,
they preach not the gospel of Calvary; there is no command to
repent (Acts 17:30), no death of Adam and resurrection in Christ

through baptism, no loving and trembling at the scriptures, no crying out for the fire of God's Spirit, no urgency to win the lost ("Is anyone lost?"), no screaming demons fleeing their blood-washed captives, no wrath and judgement Day coming the other side of the veil. "Just water it all down in the name of love, tolerance, modernity and relevance. And do not sound like a religious fanatic."

But you will hear the sheep cladding call to "love" in these sanctuaries; equality and victimisation will be huge themes. Be under no illusion: the devil is preaching fake love today. "There shan't be any preaching of the gospel on the streets thank you . . . evangelism is arrogant, judgmental, disturbs the peace and implies people have a sin-problem, a death-problem and a judgement-Day-coming problem."

No, there's little holy reverence for God, His word and His propitiation in these social (justice) clubs – mostly a carnal, consumer-driven, insipid, Baal-bowing sexuality and pagan morality with a powerless, genderless, trinket god of convenience. Whilst Jesus cries "You must be born again", here the echo is that of a Beatles pop concert – "All you need is love." Small wonder the media and press are either ignoring, laughing at or patronising with praise large sections of the spineless, saltless church of the West. Their preachers might become quasi-celebrities, but they will not be writing epistles to their congregations from the courtrooms or prisons.

It's time for the awe of God, true love and the real Jesus to replace the Disney one, return to His church and walk the streets of our cities. The Lamb of God shed His precious blood for more than this.

DAY 31
TOUGH LOVE
PART 2

*"Indeed the safest road to Hell is the gradual
one – the gentle slope, soft underfoot,
without milestones, without signposts."*

C.S. Lewis

Jesus commands His army to "Preach the gospel to all creation"
(Mark 16:15). Wow, what a royal commission! Immersed in the
Holy Ghost and fire power, we are to hit the rooftops, the streets,
the lanes, the highways, the hedges, "the media" (my addition)
to compel the lost to come in that His house might be full.

Now, preaching can take different forms but one thing it must
do is go public, incessantly. That's where the lost people are. So
is this what our Christian lives look like? My impression is that
large parts of the western church (I generalise) retreat to the
nave on a Sunday morning and asks, "is there a plan B?"

Paul writes that we are are called to judge the church
(1 Corinthians 5). The truth is I am gripped, heartbroken, angry,
at how much we seem to have traded the heroic, adventurous,
truth-heralding, sacrificial Christianity of the New Testament
for a bland, comfortable and harmless "churchianity" that so
easily fits in. I feel as if I cannot go another day without national
church repentance, revival and the healing of our land. Just this
weekend my friends and I were thrown out of a leisure centre in
Cornwall for gently telling an old lady that "Jesus loves you." The
staff at reception accused us of harassing her and ordered us
out of the building. I asked staff members if we could talk to her
about football instead. No reply. No eye contact.

Our nation is in dire straits. It is time for large scale spiritual
revolution.

If you needed any reminder that the Almighty God of the New Testament, not merely Old Testament, is not to be parlayed with or glibly passed over, then ask Ananias and Saphira (Acts 5). These two were born again believers, part of the early church, disciples of Jesus, offering money to the work of the church. But they lied in their giving and both dropped down dead on the spot by the power of the Holy Spirit. We need a fresh revelation on the holiness of God and His righteous judgement. It's going to come at us like a freight train in any case on the Great Day, whether we like it or not. So wisdom is to have died before you die. Love warns, as well as comforts.

In my opinion the enemy to the faith at the moment is liberal rebellion that waters down and compromises the absolute truths of God on the altar of political acceptability and the fear of man. This heaps up deceived teachers who teach doctrines of demons (1 Timothy 4) and the commandments of men, who make a golden calf of Jesus to suit the lusts of their flesh. These men win one proselyte and make him twice as much a son of hell as themselves and accuse the faithful of being legalistic and lacking compassion.

Paul Washer writes, *"People tell me 'judge not, lest ye be judged. I tell them, 'twist not the scripture, lest ye be like Satan."*

John Piper writes, "The world does not need cool Christians who are culturally saturated. It needs exiles with the scent of heaven and the aroma of Christ."

DAY 32
TOUGH LOVE
PART 3

"Christ did not die to redeem a Bride who would keep Him on the porch while she watched television in the den. His will for the church is that we open the door; all the doors of our life. He wants to join you in the dining room, spread a meal out for you and eat with you and talk with you. The opposite of lukewarmness is the fervour you experience when you enjoy a candlelit dinner with Jesus Christ in the innermost room of your heart. And when Jesus Christ, the sources of all God's creation, is dining with you in your heart then you will have all the gold, all the garments and all the medicine in the world."

John Piper

Compassion is a deep and strong drive of love from the gut that loves in truth, that is mature, that is sacrificial, that is willing to take a beating for the salvation, the eternal good of their neighbour. "To live is Christ to die is gain." Church! We have forgotten why we are born again. Our lives are not our own. "Is there not a cause?", cried David to the army of Israel petrified before Goliath. We have sold our birth right for a comfortable bowl of soup. It doesn't matter whether you are standing inside the furnace or outside of the furnace. It doesn't matter if the authorities are making things seven times hotter, it only matters that you went with Jesus and that He is standing next to you.

Never compromise faithfulness for worldly comfort. It's a mirage. The end is misery. For what profit is it to a man if he gains the whole world, and loses his own soul? Never sacrifice the anointing for respectability with man. Andrew Foster writes, *"We must shout the whole counsel of the gospel from the rooftops. Our politically correct, over sensitive, conformist society has permeated our air-conditioned churches with a lukewarmness of the Laodicean church."* We are warned in scripture that lukewarm Christianity makes the Lord spew us out His mouth (Revelation 3:16). And so, it ought to make us sick also. Those He loves He rebukes and chastens. May we repent and be zealous. May people see in our blazing lives the evidence of an encounter with the living God.

It goes on to say in Acts 5:12-13, *"And through the hands of the apostles many signs and wonders were done among the people. And they were all with one accord in Solomon's Porch. Yet none of the rest dared join them, but the people esteemed them highly."* I am afraid we are so desperate to be relevant, that we are oceans away from the high esteem that makes people hardly dare join His holy church. May our carnal slumber, idolatry and hiding cease and those days of authentic, sacrificial, zealous, white-hot ecclesiastic glory return to these lands, so help us God.

DAY 33
THE BEAUTY OF BROKENNESS

"The Lord disciplines those he loves."
Hebrew 12:6

Have you ever watched a wild horse be broken in so that it can be ridden successfully? It's violent, it's messy, it isn't easy. Unyielded, unharnessed, wilful strength dies hard. But the end result is majestic. Part of the chastening process that the Father must take all His children through (Hebrews 12:5-11) is the breaking of the flesh – breaking our reliance on our own self-sufficiency to make things happen. This is the way of the orphaned world, even religion, the way we have been taught to live independent from God – by law instead of grace.

This is also why "burn out", even some break downs, although painful, can serve as beautiful new chapters in life, particularly if the root of the problem was living independently from God and the fruit new intimacy with the Father, freedom, rest and miraculously-authored exploits. The Bible is full of very real characters that were led on a journey out of their own strength and initiative and into God's, often painfully. Some of the pain was of their making and some was authored by God, but in the latter instance always and only unto a higher, freer, more glorious end. God is only ever good, although His ways are higher than ours.

Abraham produced Ishmael through Hagar because he couldn't trust God to produce an heir. Abraham was then tested by God with Isaac to see if he would really fear and trust Him alone (Genesis 22). Jacob the "deceiver" wrestled with God and became Israel ("Prince") walking the rest of his days with a limp but with royal identity. Martha was busy, anxious, resentful, apparently serving God in her own strength and was told by Jesus that only "one thing" (sitting at His feet) was needed, whilst zealous Saul murdered Christians in service to God before being struck blind by (the same) God to become the now "seeing" Paul the Apostle.

Any "breaking" which breaks our reliance on self and reduces us to the walk of grace, which brings an end to our perpetual doing, engineering, earning and achieving things for God in our own strength is not only a good thing, it's essential if we are to have any lasting peace and reward in eternity (1 Corinthians 3:10-15). We are not called to do things for God, we are called to a life of intimacy, relationship, ecstatic yieldedness and a light yoke where Christ lives His powerful life through us. As Steve Mcvey writes, "Not only does Christ call us to the Christian life, but He will also live it for us. Resting in Christ is the sole responsibility of the Christian. Everything else flows out of that."

DAY 34
YOU ARE COVERED

*"For who makes you differ from another? And
what do you have that you did not receive?
Now if you did indeed receive it, why do you
boast as if you had not received it?"*
1 Corinthians 4:7

Pride. Shame. Humility.

Pride and shame are egocentric, two sides of the same, orphan "coin", where "self" is king. Pride fuels vain-glory, envy and comparison, whereas humility lives for God's glory and celebrates others' success. Shame leads to hiding, breeds perfectionism and calls me to compete with others unnecessarily, frantically dressing my nakedness with the "fig leaves" of worldly accolade. In contrast, humility is unselfconscious, team-focused, happy to be "last". My significance and worth have been settled elsewhere. (John 13:1-5)

Strongholds of pride and shame in a person's life lead to hypocrisy, posturing, man-pleasing and a performance mind-set. When I am ashamed or proud I am also easily offended. My insecurity (wrong security) makes me defensive for I have placed, perhaps subconsciously, my identity and justification in my own performance. Consequently, I am compelled to protect my ego on the one hand, or hide my shame on the other.

You cannot humiliate a truly humble person. Perfect love has cast out fear. The self has been crucified. The focus is now outward. If you mock and squeeze humility, love comes out. Behold the naked, beaten, taunted and exposed Christ: *"Father, forgive them, for they know no what they do."* (Luke 23:34)

The humble, whilst knowing they have no righteousness of their own, have fully received, embraced and celebrate the righteousness of Calvary. The cross has become their only boast (Galatians 6:11-15). They have nothing to protect. They are adopted, heaven's very own, sons and daughters, children of the Most High God.

Humility yields rested, selfless, hiddenness in Christ. I have become one with Love, covered by His robe alone (Luke 15). Now I am no longer touchy, over-sensitive, defensive, nor easily offended. I no longer need to take myself so seriously, for "self" is no longer at the centre of things – I know I am deeply, unconditionally loved by my Father. And so, humility shuns all hypocrisy and leads to transparent, unguarded living, integrity, authenticity, lightness, fun and laughter. The pressure is off.

True humility is not thinking of yourself any better or worse than another. *"For who makes you differ from another?"* All is precious grace. Humble authenticity is the enemy of shame and pride. A right revelation of the cross and gracious, unconditional love both from heaven and between people is the healer for us all. Remember, your nakedness has been covered eternally. In Christ, you are righteous.

DAY 35
THE BEAUTY OF WILDERNESS
PART 1

*"My temptations have been my
Masters of Divinity."*
Martin Luther

The wilderness has very bad press but, ironically (Hebrews 12:11), great fruit. I am finally coming to see wilderness as beautiful. It is vital to understand that as children of God, no trial is wasted, no season left without purpose and without promise. "*He makes everything beautiful in its time*" (Ecclesiastes 3:11). Wilderness and trial are essential seasons in God's calendar. And although God is only good and never author of evil, the Holy Spirit uses it all, leading us both in and out.

Jesus went through a wilderness, Israel went through it, Abraham, Jacob, Joseph, Moses, King David . . . The list is long and distinguished. In the wilderness, God gently exposes the issues of our hearts, so that with our co-operation, He can graciously remove them and set us free.

In the wilderness, Jesus was assaulted by the devil with regard to His true identity. Take time to meditate on Matthew 4.

The wilderness forces the question. Who are you, really? Is your identity a by-product of your activity and usefulness ("satisfy your immediate need, make bread, perform miracles") or will you accept your place as the beloved and find life in relationship and obedience? Will you believe who God says you are, your portion in Him and rest alone in that? Or is sonship and royalty not enough? The wilderness has a crafty way of exposing whether Jesus is Lord of our lives or butler to our desires and ego.

This perfect Father has so much more for us than what our flesh craves and what the world tells us we need. God loves us where we are but way too much to leave us in the shallows.

"And have you [completely] forgotten the divine word of appeal and encouragement in which you are reasoned with and addressed as sons? You must submit to and endure [correction] for discipline; God is dealing with you as with sons."

(Hebrews 12:5,7)

The writer of Hebrews appeals to our remembrance. Where is your focus? What is your attitude to life, wilderness and trial? Kathryn Kuhlman said, "Whether life grinds a man down or polishes him depends on what he's made of." When we have the right (biblical) attitude we realise that the wilderness is God's kindness, forming Christ in His children and making Himself pre-eminent in our hearts. The wilderness takes us from the spiritual bondage of orphan-hearted restlessness and joyless carnality, to a life of peace and joy in the spirit of adoption. The wilderness frees us from being a victim to circumstance to being content in any situation. Often we are drawn away from what we thought we wanted to what we really need, what we were truly fashioned for. The wilderness forms a bedrock of character to then house the true desires of our hearts safely.

DAY 36
THE BEAUTY OF WILDERNESS
PART 2

*"While Christianity was able to agree with pagan
writers that inordinate attachment to earthly
goods can lead to unnecessary pain and grief, it
also taught that the answer to this was not to love
things less but to love God more than anything else.
Only when our greatest love is God, a love that we
cannot lose even in death, can we face all things
with peace. Grief was not to be eliminated but
seasoned and buoyed up with love and hope."*

Tim Keller

Will your trust in the goodness of God, your confession of faith, be ruled by circumstance and feeling or by the word of God? How ruthless is your "It is written" response to what is happening around you? Steve Backlund said, *"God likes to send people to deserts to teach them how to repent. To change the way we think."* The desert yields the godly sorrow without which there is no true repentance, no true freedom.

See how God tenderly exhorts His people, Israel:

"The Lord your God who brought you out of the land of Egypt, from the house of bondage; who led you through that great and terrible wilderness, in which were fiery serpents and scorpions and thirsty land where there was no water; who brought water for you out of the flinty rock; who fed you in the wilderness with manna, which your fathers did not know, that He might humble you and that He might test you, to do you good in the end."

(Deuteronomy 8:14-16)

"For the Lord your God is bringing you into a good land, a land of brooks of water, of fountains and springs, flowing forth in valleys and hills . . . And beware lest you say in your [mind and] heart, My power and the might of my hand have gotten me this wealth."

(Deuteronomy 8:7, 17)

The wilderness humbles the flesh. This is so we can be free of the exhaustion of the flesh and glorify in the riches that God gives freely and God alone sustains.

Lastly, but perhaps most importantly, ecstatic intimacy with God thrives in the wilderness. Our dependence on God sparks deepening romance with God and thirst for His presence alone. *"Who is this coming up from the wilderness, leaning upon her beloved?"* (Song of Songs 8:5). Have you become one who has the delightful life of leaning?

The wilderness is very good news if we will see it from God's perspective and rest in His sovereign grace. Don't waste your trials. Let God deal with your heart, that's where His attention is fixed. Don't continue around the same mountain time and time again. Come out of the wilderness glistening with romance, grace and power.

DAY 37
WAITING IN STILLNESS

"All of humanity's problems stem from man's inability to sit quietly in a room alone."

Blaise Pascal

To move in the opposite spirit of the smart phone addiction generation, we must cultivate the spacious place of stillness of heart. We must learn to wait, be present and indulge the naked now, in all its quietness, stillness, awkwardness and discomfort.

Cultivate blessed communion with God in solitude. Paul Tillich noted, *"Loneliness is the pain of being alone, solitude is the glory of being alone."*

We must learn to sit with ourselves. Sit with another person in the quietness. Wait on God, wait on people around you, wait with yourself, resist the endorphin-fix of the trivial. "Busyness is maybe the most vocation – destroying condition there is," writes Eugene Peterson. Leanness of soul is the inheritance of the perpetually busy. You are worth more than that. Listen for the wind or the birdsong.

Waiting has become a despised virtue in our microwave, Amazon Prime, information-obese generation. Your spirit only wants revelation. Waiting is not painful, it's deepening and enriching if we'll enter into trust, thanksgiving for the glory that is already right there and learn to wonder again. Waiting on God yields spiritual joy – from His face pours forth light. How wretched we are to replace His face for the LED so easily. Restlessness, lust, shallow spirituality and fear of missing out is the realm of the orphan. Rest and peace is the realm of God and His children. May we be set apart, caught away in romance once again.

This is what the Sovereign Lord, the Holy One of Israel, says: *"In repentance and rest is your salvation, in quietness and trust is your strength, but you would have none of it."*

(Isaiah 30:15)

DAY 38
FIGHT BY REST

"Therefore, since a promise remains of
entering His rest, let us fear lest any
of you seem to have come short of it."

Hebrews 4:1

Rest is the realm of God. Rest is violence to darkness. The only place where the Lord tells His people to fear is fear that we do not enter His rest.

Are you at rest today? Are you present? Or are you anxiously thinking ahead, worrying about the future, consumed by 'destination disease' ("One day I will be happy when . . .") or regretfully chewing on past mistakes? So many people are restless, unable to be present with people or present with the Lord. The Lord has rest for us.

When we hear the gospel, the word of God, we must mix it with faith, stand on it.

"For indeed the gospel was preached to us as well as to them; but the word which they heard did not profit them, not being mixed with faith in those who heard it. For we who have believed do enter that rest . . . the works were finished from the foundation of the world."

(Hebrews 4:2-3)

How do you enter rest? Believe! Say to your situation, I choose to believe the invisible, not the visible, I believe that God's works for my life have been finished, I believe the "it is finished" of Calvary, that I am enough, flawless, in perfect relationship with God, through Jesus' finished work, in spite of my performance. I am the righteousness of God in Christ.

Feasting on truth, right believing, coming into trust and rest, is real warfare. When you feast on God's word you fight. Why? Because faith comes from feasting and faith is our victory.

This is the victory that conquers the world, even our faith.

"Who is it that is victorious over [that conquers] the world but he who believes that Jesus is the Son of God [who adheres to, trusts in, and relies on that fact]?"

(1 John 5:4-5)

He prepares a table (of feasting) before us in the presence of our enemies.

Faith is what destroys Satan. "Only believe". You fight by not fighting. You fight by rest. Rest, through trust, is holy terrorism. Orphans strive and they must maintain, sons inherit. The deepest manifestation of sonship is rest, through trust.

"Then David said to the Philistine, "You come to me with a sword, with a spear, and with a javelin. But I come to you in the name of the Lord of hosts, the God of the armies of Israel, whom you have defied."
(1 Samuel 17:45)

David recognised that Goliath came with the visible, but that God's people must come with the invisible. Goliath came with the temporal, the limited, David came with the eternal, the omnipotent. That alone was his victory.

"Fight the good fight of faith, saints!"   (1 Timothy 6:12)

Here are five words of happy grace for you today: "The battle is the Lord's."

DAY 39
ABRAHAM'S LAUGHTER

*"Faith, mighty faith, the promise sees, and
looks to God alone; Laughs at impossibilities,
and cries it shall be done."*

Charles Wesley

Medalling with Hagar or trusting with Sarah. This is a prophetic picture of all of our lives. Over 25 years of turbulent waiting and testing Abraham learned that there was nothing he could do to cook up his inheritance. When he moved in the flesh it led to jealousy, strife and the child, Ishmael, born out of slavery. *"Oh that Ishmael might live before You!"* (Genesis 17:18). The fruit of Abram's efforts (for that was still his name) wasn't blessed. Freedom came through covenant inheritance, when Abram had given up. God did what He had always promised, what was naturally impossible for an old man and barren woman aged 100.

Paul put it like this:

*"The person who lives in right relationship with God does it
by embracing what God arranges for him. Doing things for
God is the opposite of entering into what God does for you."*

Galatians 3:12-14 (MSG)

Remember what Isaiah wrote:

*"Rejoice, barren woman who bears no children, shout
and cry out, woman who has no birth pangs, Because the
children of the barren woman now surpass the children of
the chosen woman."*

(Isaiah 54:1, Galatians 4:27)

Isaac means laughter. With the birth of Isaac, Abraham finally became heir of the promise (covenant circumcision came through Isaac, Genesis 17). Both he and Sarah entered their promised land of laughing, joyful rest. None of us will have rest apart from the new covenant in Jesus' blood. Through one child alone, Abraham became Father of many nations.

Abram became Abraham as God worked meekness in Him. It took 25 years of character sifting. Like Abraham, our spiritual journey is from the "Ishmaels" of orphan-hearted striving to the impossible, inward-"laughter"-inheritance of covenant Isaac (Genesis 17). Grace. The question is not "God, what can I do for you?", but "Father, what do you want to give me and do in and through me?" Heirs, as opposed to employees, have learned to receive His promises as His children. They have finally let go of control and chosen a life of rested, impossibility-crushing laughter. Let's forsake the striving of the flesh, live by the Spirit, and trust God to birth nations through our barrenness. This is the gospel of grace.

DAY 40
LIVING LIKE A KING

"It isn't Narnia, you know," sobbed Lucy. "It's
you. We shan't meet you there. And how
can we live, never meeting you?"
"But you shall meet me, dear one," said Aslan.
"Are you there too, Sir?" said Edmund.
"I am," said Aslan. "But there I have another
name. You must learn to know me by that name.
This was the very reason why you were brought
to Narnia, that by knowing me here for a little,
you may know me better there."

C.S. Lewis, The Voyage of the Dawn Treader

I am having a pot of Earl Grey tea (18 Euros a tea bag it seems) on the roof terrace of the Danieli, the most famous hotel in Venice. I have been shown around the royal suite, which is available tonight at 9,000 Euros (without breakfast) in case I feel too exhausted to get my train back to the countryside. I enjoy seeing the best the world has to offer, mainly because I love excellence, as a child of the King I'm allowed it, can receive and enjoy it without deserving it, and lastly, often so that I can disrobe it of its occasional posturing, pomp and ultimate vanity.

Having carefully inspected Danieli's best, an observation: Royalty is an inside job, not a room number or a family name. True royalty is Jesus or the unsullied outworking of Christ in and through me. The real hotel suite or home you sleep in is your heart. You can lie in the most luxurious and enormous bed in the Danieli, but if your conscience is a pigsty, your soul small and grimy, your aspirations lean, self-centred and godless, it doesn't matter whether you are in the Danieli royal, or the penthouse at the Ritz, you are living far from your royal call. Guard the palace that is your heart, for that is where your real life comes from.

May we turn things on their head? As we provide a suite for Father, Son and Holy Spirit, by grace royalty comes. Not only will we begin to experience royal contentment, peace, joy, whatever our outward circumstances (the inferior reality) but circumstance will bend to our spiritual reality (the superior). We'll see different, the "Instagram" filter will change. Then we will be transformed from victimized thermometer to powerful, atmosphere shifting thermostat.

The perpetual presence of the King of kings in our humble suite will deepen our relationships to five star integrity and those quiet desperations of our former lusts for vain existential gains will be swallowed up in divine intimacy and eternal purpose. Show the Lord round your suite. Give Him all access. He won't hesitate to take over the place.

DAY 41
MAN UP, CHURCH!
PART 1

"But God doesn't call us to be comfortable. He calls us to trust Him completely so that we are unafraid to put ourselves in situations where we will be in trouble if He doesn't come through"

Francis Chan

To call Jesus your Saviour implies that you are saved from something. If you are "saved" then your life, in large part, is about getting the lost saved. In fact, your participation in this eternity-shaking commission is the evidence that the Spirit of God has possessed you. What an honour.

Is there any greater privilege than reconciling man to God? You are not now treading the earth to come back under the death slumber of the world – an impressive job, a tasty pad, enviable slacks, an honourable reputation amongst all who meet you. You are separated unto the Lord. You are commissioned into the perishing sea of humanity to save drowning souls! "Come, follow Me, and I will make you fishers of men." (Matthew 4:19)

Quoting Jesus, William Macdonald wrote this: *"If anyone desires to come after Me, let him deny himself, and take up his cross . . ."* (Matthew 16:24) The cross is not some physical infirmity or mental anguish; these things are common to all men. The cross is a pathway that is deliberately chosen. It is, as C. A. Coates put it, *"a path which so far as this world goes is one of dishonour and reproach."* The cross symbolises the shame, persecution and abuse which the world heaped on the Son of God, and which the world will heap on all who choose to stand against the tide. Any believer can avoid the cross simply by being conformed to the world and its ways."

148

Let's take a quick tour through the pages of scripture and wonder at the end of some of our heroes:

Isaiah was sawn in two with a wooden saw. Amos was tortured and afterwards slain. Habakkuk was stoned by the Jews in Jerusalem. Jeremiah was stoned by the Jews in Egypt, because he rebuked them for worshipping idols. Ezekiel was slain by the chief of the Jews, because he rebuked him for worshipping idols.

Zechariah the son of Berachiah, the priest, was from Jerusalem. Joash, the king slew this prophet between the steps and the altar, and sprinkled his blood upon the horns of the altar, and the priests buried him. From that day God forsook the temple and angels were never seen again in it.

The first apostles – Andrew: Martyrdom by crucifixion (bound, not nailed, to a cross). Bartholomew (often identified with Nathaniel in the New Testament): Martyrdom either by being 1. Beheaded or 2. Flayed alive and crucified, head downward. James the Greater: Martyrdom by being beheaded or stabbed with a sword. James the Lesser: Martyrdom by being thrown from a pinnacle of the Temple at Jerusalem, then stoned and beaten with clubs. Jude (often identified with Thaddeus in the New Testament): Martyrdom by being beaten to death with a club. Matthew: Martyrdom by being burned, stoned, or beheaded. Peter: Martyrdom by crucifixion at Rome with his head downwards. Philip: Martyrdom. Simon: Martyrdom by crucifixion. or being sawn in half. Thomas: Martyrdom by being stabbed with a spear.

Stephen was stoned to death. Paul was likely beheaded in Rome. Lastly, our Master: Jesus went about tipping idols, poking strongholds and shaking cages. Jesus was beaten within inches of His life then crucified by Pilate via the protests of the chief priests. True love got Jesus killed in the end, even though it was He who laid His own life down.

A servant is not above his Master. Grant us courage, Lord.

DAY 42
MAN UP, CHURCH!
PART 2

*"Courage is not simply one of the virtues, but the
form of every virtue at testing point."*

C.S. Lewis

There is a man-pleasing, platitudinous idolatry passed off as 'Christian wisdom'. This stops the Daniels of our day from speaking out and being thrown to the lions – the consequence of which produces outrageous miracles, the repentance of kings and the releasing of entire nations from slavery. Babylon never has the last laugh – her lion's den is the gateway to national revival. If you do a study from the New Testament of characteristics of people filled with the Holy Spirit, you will find two chilling traits. John the Baptist (filled from birth), Jesus, Peter, Paul and Stephen were all:

1. People of plain speech.
2. Martyred.

In other words, the Holy Spirit doesn't endorse woolly talk. He is never political.

Mark Batterson writes:

"I wonder if our culture of political correctness has left us too thin skinned. Again, I'm not advocating for careless, thoughtless, heartless insults. But when political correctness becomes the Golden Rule, speaking truth becomes bigotry. Truth is crucified in the name of tolerance, undermining civil debate, conscientious objection, and religious conviction.

We live in a culture where it's wrong to say something is wrong. And I think that's wrong! Remaining silent on a thing that God has spoken about isn't loving – it's cowardly. And when we fail to use our voice, we lose our voice. We as the church should be more known for what we're for than what we're against. But playing the man requires standing up for what you believe in, even if you're standing alone.

A few diagnostic questions: When was the last time you were criticised? If it's been a while, it should make you nervous. Why? Because it probably means you're maintaining the status quo rather than challenging it. You can't make a difference without making waves, and some people in the boat won't like it. So be it. Rock the boat anyway. Also, how easily offended are you? If the answer is easily, then you need to man up. When you take offence, you become defensive. And the second you become defensive, the kingdom of God stops advancing through you."

(Excerpt taken from Play the Man)

Jim Elliot (1927-1956) was one of five missionaries killed while participating in Operation Auca, an attempt to evangelise the Huaorani people of Ecuador. Jim prayed this; *"Father, make of me a crisis man. Bring those I contact to decision. Let me not be a milepost on a single road; make me a fork, that men must turn one way or another on facing Christ in me."*

If you are a born-again believer, an ambassador for heaven, the cross-shaped life of sacrificial love that you are called into makes you His crisis man or woman. Do you accept?

DAY 43
PLURALISM AND MULTI-FAITH ISSUES

"I am the way, the truth and the life.
No one comes to the Father except through Me."

John 14:6

A brief note on pluralism and multi-faith issues: it is not a noble quality for born again believers to be uncritical of other religions. On the contrary, the fact that one is born again through Christ implies that every other 'way' to God leaves a man dead in sin (Ephesians 2:1). Or did the Christ die in vain (Galatians 2:21)?

The Bible is clear that every other religion and god is idolatry. Demonstrating honour, love and kindness towards people need not and must not compromise truth. I must criticize and expose idolatry and false religion wisely and graciously but also unashamedly and in the truth.

Love doesn't paper over eternal fault lines. Loving the person will always involve hating the sin. Sin enslaves, robs life and destroys destiny. Hating the sin rightly, will always involve loving the person unconditionally and choosing to bless those who hate and persecute in return.

Lord, grant us wisdom and courage in the timing and rhythm of Your Spirit.

DAY 44
THE FULL STORY

*"Tell me in the light of the cross, isn't it a scandal
that you and I live today as we do."*
Alan Redpath

There is nothing token or cute about Christianity. There's nothing in the original script that makes Jesus suitable for a couple of public holidays per year.

What I am about to comment on people generally don't like reading about today. Thankfully, God is not subject to our tastes and the word of God doesn't pander to our convenience, political manoeuvrings, carnal comforts (He's after a comfort far deeper), nor the grotesque and blasphemous perversions of some of the ministers in the church. If it did, Jesus wouldn't have been killed and He wouldn't have risen from the dead. And we would have no good news to speak of. No, we need the full story.

We like words like mercy, love, grace, forgiveness, redemption, resurrection, heaven. Thank God these themes and truths are woven into His gospel and intrinsic to His beautiful character. Aren't you grateful that the God of the universe is the paragon of virtue and the giver of ultimate love and hope?

But we must also face and embrace other doctrines, no less true, like sin, wrath, judgment, punishment and hell fire. These realities and doctrines are epidemic throughout the scriptures, and when held up alongside a fallen world marred with unrepentant murder, abuse, lust, injustice, corruption and innocent suffering, they make for reason and ultimate vindication. Someone once said "How can a God of love send people to hell?" Another said, "When you consider 70 million people murdered under Hitler and Stalin, with Nazi officers looking upon hanging bodies of women in laughter, how can a God of love not send people to hell?"

The gospel is visceral, bloody, appalling, stunning. The harrowing but wonderful news is that Jesus Christ exhausted the wrath and judgment of Almighty God at Calvary. And that wrath and judgment was pointed at the sin in all of us. We're all guilty. Jesus became sin that we might become the righteousness of God in Him, by faith. God put on skin, only to have it torn off Him in shreds by His own rebellious creation as the literal scapegoat and Mediator for His lost children.

Dry ritual can anaesthetize what, at first, apprehends entirely; we must remember that when the church takes communion she celebrates and feasts on sacrificial torture unto salvation and divine intimacy. The veil is now torn, once, for all. All can enter into the presence of God boldly by the blood of Jesus alone. It's not the stuff of fairytales. It's so much grittier, more offensive and real. And, thus, believable.

Jesus then rose from the dead as the scriptures predicted and His ragtag group of disciples turned the known world upside down. Either you accept Jesus as your personal Lord and Saviour or you meet with God's wrath and righteous judgement, without an Advocate. I wouldn't wish that on my worst enemy.

God is love, full of mercy, slow to anger, rich in love. But He is also God – He will not be parleyed with; there's no "discussing of terms", He doesn't run a democracy and He doesn't sit in on our neurotic committees. He is God. He is King outright. He is holy. If the word of God failed, if He were fickle like us, the universe would implode (Hebrews 1:3). Let God be true and every man and devil a liar.

It is finished. "Kiss the Son or receive His wrath" (Psalm 2:12). Come humbly and receive His mercy through Jesus while you can, or stay proud and take His eternal judgment. No-one is escaping hell or entering into heaven without being washed in the blood of Jesus. There's no other way God can accept sinners and remain a just God.

"Behold the Lamb of God who takes away the sin of the world."

DAY 45
JUSTICE IN ORDER

" If you want to meet the needs of the poor
in this world, there is no better place to
start than by preaching the gospel."

K.P. Yohannan

I would like to suggest that social justice is a beautiful fruit of the gospel, a terrible replacement. In truth, biblical justice needs no prefix. It's all justice to God. "Righteousness and justice are the foundation of His throne" (Psalm 97:2). The point I wish to address here is that social justice has fast become a replacement for the cross of Jesus the world over (particularly in the west) and even in large parts of the church. Today, freeing sex slaves (an awesome call) might get you an MBE, whereas calling for repentance on abortion, "worse" preaching repentance to homosexuals might land you in prison.

The world will applaud and fund social justice warriors. This can be a great thing. But when it is used as a replacement for His cross, to feed and placate our craving for self-righteous immortality, the fruit stinks to God. When the church uses social justice because it is more socially acceptable than preaching the gospel, that, too, is idolatry. Remember, friendship with the world is enmity with God. That doesn't mean that God doesn't applaud social justice, He *longs* for justice in every way (Isaiah 58), but it does mean that He is looking at our motivations, counting how many souls are getting born again and ready for heaven in the process (Luke 15). Who will fund the "scum of the earth" evangelical missionaries? (Paul's words in 1 Corinthians 4:13 MSG)

"Rather rejoice because your names are written in heaven" (Luke 10:20). The church's primary call is to preach a repentance and forgiveness, heaven-and-hell gospel (Mark 16). The gospel also wars against social injustice. The cause of the poor, human trafficking, the life of the unborn, domestic abuse, gender inequality

(remembering that men and women are wonderfully different) and racial hatred are all at the heart of God's plan for redemption, heaven restored in the earth.

JJ Waters (Director, Kingdom Impact Framework) said this: "When the gospel is valued highly enough and in its right place theologically, social justice can make a great entry point for it – I am seeing this with many of the organisations I am working with. Sometimes Jesus led with proclamation, other times demonstration."

Jesus said this: "Let your light so shine before men, that they may see your good works and glorify your Father in heaven." (Matthew 5:16) Our demonstration of the gospel through justice causes can point people to God and His gospel. But we need to understand that right now the Jezebel spirit of intimidation in the world wants the church cowering from her primary call of preaching the gospel. She wants us silent, saltless, blunt, harmless. So, she is offering a worthy replacement, as opposed to "consummation", in social justice causes. To the less discerning the devil comes disguised as an angel of light, ensuring that the good becomes the enemy of the best.

The gospel of repentance alone offends the self-righteous rebel. So, Jezebel seduces the spineless Ahab-church with social justice causes (apart from salvation from sin) which ultimately reduce the church to a fake, humanistic mission. When the church capitulates, she is in deep sin and man-fearing bondage. Preach the gospel with your life and also with your necessary and obedient voice – that's righteousness. Remember the cross, remember the poor.

In truth, the church must crave both eternal justice through the preaching of the gospel and social justice as we move out into society. Each may bud from either, when our hearts are right before God. But let the second commandment come by the empowerment of the first. Then these weapons become mutually complimentary. Let's press into the full reward of Jesus, the whole remit of God's heart and hand in this hour. The proclaimed gospel of heaven and hell in our hearts central, Jesus Christ crucified and raised from the dead to save sinners, and the gospel of social justice, health justice (healing and deliverance) and every other divine justice accomplished at Calvary, coming strong alongside.

DAY 46
GOD WITH ME

*"Fear not, for I am with you; be not dismayed, for I
am your God; I will strengthen you, I will help you,
I will uphold you with my righteous right hand."*

Isaiah 41:10

I like to call the tree of knowledge: the tree of independence,
the tree of pressure and the tree of self. The fruit is fear, control,
death. Fear arises when I imagine that everything depends
on me. My orphan wiring and history easily loads pressure on
myself. I have slipped back into the heavy yoke that the world
loads upon me. After all, back then, I was ultimately alone.

But then I remember my new creation reality. I remember
communion. I return. The prison of self (with all its exhausting
justifications and empty righteousness) is swallowed up in happy
sonship, His righteousness, His plan for my life and His working.
This is the tree of Life. There are always two trees in the garden.
Jesus, the tree of Life, comes full of grace and truth, setting
me free to rest. Faith and joy arise as I remember that God is
always with me. I can depend and lean on Him every time and
all the time.

DAY 47
TWO ROADS

*"Enter by the narrow gate; for wide is the gate and
broad is the way that leads to destruction,
and there are many who go in by it. Because
narrow is the gate and difficult is the way which
leads to life, and there are few who find it."*
Jesus (Matthew 7:13-14)

Everyone reading this is in a spiritual battle. You may be currently living "well", have a large family and a fancy house but there is a war going on for your soul. And eternity is only one faulty heartbeat away for you. You may be a student, or fresh out of university "without a care in the world", but the truth is you have a foe who wants to kill, steal and destroy from your life, your true destiny and drag you to hell. There is a devil, he is a deceiver, most people don't believe he exists (even many in the church of Jesus hardly acknowledge him) and that perhaps is the greatest trick he has ever pulled.

But the great news is that there is a loving Father, a Saviour Jesus Christ and an empowering Holy Sprit to guide you through life, give you true meaning and eternal purpose, peace, joy and His righteousness by faith. God is for you! He is waiting for all His children with open arms and royal garments.

Everyone reading this has been born once. You didn't choose that. But you must be born again to be made ready for heaven. These are the words of Jesus Christ and this second (spiritual) birth is your choice. It's the only way anyone will have eternal life and escape the wrath and judgement of a holy God that is coming on sin. Now you may not like the sound of that but let me be clear with you (as most aren't) because I love you- the cross of Calvary is not moved by your offense, nor your self-righteous indignation. The spilt blood of Jesus Christ cannot be taken back. It can only be drunk with deep, humble gratitude or proudly spurned. Which line are you in?

Lavish grace, mercy, complete forgiveness, abundant life and the wonderful infilling of the Holy Spirit is available today for the humble and repentant through Christ Jesus. Or you can be a slave to the demonic realm. Jesus Christ, the perfect representation of God, was crucified at Calvary and judged in our place to make atonement for human sin, mine and yours, was buried and three days later He rose from the dead. Jesus is alive, now seated at the right hand of the Almighty and you can (and must) know Him intimately and follow Him wonderfully. But He will soon come as Judge of all. Are you ready?

> *"I will dismantle the wisdom of the wise and I will invalidate the intelligence of the scholars."*
>
> (1 Corinthians 1:19 TPT)

Now, you may not get this news on the BBC, CNN, in The Daily Mail, the lauded lecture halls of the Ivy League universities, or even (sadly) from the brassy lectern of your local church, but I assure you as God is my daily witness, as the scripture is unbreakable, as hundreds of millions of simple, former lost souls will testify, this is the truest, most beautiful news you will ever hear. And the most important.

Many people have bought the lie that there is no God, that truth is relative, that man is not ultimately accountable to his Maker, that this earth is some sort of cosmic accident. They have bought the lie that their "cultural decency" somehow qualifies them for a heaven of their choosing and making. Seduced by and drunk on western idolatry, great multitudes are spiritually dead, concerned only by their next mortgage repayment, job promotion, Tinder date, or Instagram-microwave-meal at the mall. We have a spiritual crisis on our plates of Second World War proportions and the alarm must be sounded without interruption.

Beloved friends. Pinch your side. Life is short, flesh is like grass, flowers in the summery field, here one day gone the next. None of us is guaranteed even tomorrow. May God bless you today to know the two paths available. To know God's love and provision in Christ Jesus that alone saves you and protects you from the way of death, damnation and the wrath which is to come (John 3:36, Mathew 3:7). I leave you with a piece from Proverbs 2 to chew on and bless you:

Proverbs 2:7-13 (TPT)

"For the Lord has a hidden storehouse of wisdom made accessible to his godly lovers. He becomes your personal bodyguard as you follow his ways, protecting and guarding you as you choose what is right.

Then you will discover all that is just, proper, and fair, and be empowered to make the right decisions as you walk into your destiny.

When wisdom wins your heart and revelation breaks in, true pleasure enters your soul.

If you choose to follow good counsel, divine design will watch over you and understanding will protect you from making poor choices.

It will rescue you from evil in disguise and from those who speak duplicities.

For they have left the highway of holiness and walk in the ways of darkness."

DAY 48
ARRIVAL VS. HOPE

"Living in abundance involves staying in your lane and thriving in the place and season God has you in."
Bill Johnson

The world tells us that one day we can "arrive". The entertainment and consumer cultures present us with a plethora of shiny montages (complete with our favourite soundtrack) of houses, holidays, cars, clothes, culinary delicacies, family, faultless romances, perfect relationships and career successes. Our sensual appetite is provoked into overload, our spiritual appetite shoved into its proper place.

With divine alignment, these things listed above can be great blessings. God is a good Father and a generous giver of good and perfect gifts! (Matthew 7:11, James 1:13) But, apart from their rightful place in God's wise, gracious calendar, they can easily act as thieves of His best. Having acquired them greedily, they can steal from His first place in our lives and the destiny He has for us to walk in. Without them, they steal from our rest and our ability to remain present, full, content In Him today. In either case, the thing is an imposter. It has become Lord. My eyes have strayed from the True Prize, the True God.

If not careful, we can very easily live with a lottery mentality; perhaps sub-consciously; we hope for some day, in the not-too-distant future, when we can sit back, relax, build bigger barns for our wealth and somehow be free of any interference from God. We are God, surrounded by our minion gods. We are safe. We have arrived.

What we fail to understand is that we are only ever satisfied in faith. Not only that but "It is more blessed to give than to receive." (Acts 20:35) We are made for trusting, child-like, generous relationship, intimacy and adventure with God and his people, not some kind of controlled, material palace of independence. We are made for love and the adventure of faith. Like Abraham, wide-eyed, happy children often don't know where they are going (Hebrews 11:8). Their perpetual today is packed with excited, free, "present-ness."

"Arrival" is an existential mirage, an empty lie, which many have painfully tasted to their detriment and despair. Those that have "made it" will tell you (if they're honest enough) when you get to the top there is nothing there. In Luke 12, Jesus tells the sobering story of a rich fool. Jesus warns us to beware covetousness because life does not consist in the abundance of possessions and that any day our soul may be required of us to give account before God.

Jesus goes on to say that life is more than food, clothes, barns, land . . . (Luke 12:13-23). With startling confidence Jesus declares that "I am the life" and the only source of life in its abundance (John 10:10, 14:6). Abundant life is not a destination or arrival. It's the Lordship and intimacy of Jesus. And true satisfaction is carrying out our divine assignment. "My food is to do the will of Him who sent Me and to finish that work." (John 4:34) God is never a side order. Jesus comes as Lord in order to take over completely and satisfy fully, or He doesn't come at all.

CS Lewis writes, *"He who has God and everything else has no more than he who has God only."* Drink that in for a moment. Let that minister to you. God made things such that every one of His children can have life in its fullness in Him apart from their earthly status. If you have Jesus, and put Him first, you have everything (Matthew 6:33). Do you believe it? The material world, even the soulish realm, is purposefully forbidden the glorious place that only God can satisfy. You are free! Throw off all the trappings of 'destination disease', material lust and worldly anchor. Enter into divine adventure with Jesus. Fix your eyes on the unfading unseen. Eternal hope with ecstatic pilgrimage, now that's something to sell everything for.

DAY 49
THE ROYAL PRIESTHOOD

*"I look on all the world as my parish; thus
far I mean, that, in whatever part of it I
am, I judge it meet, right, and my bounden
duty, to declare unto all that are willing
to hear, the glad tidings of salvation."*

John Wesley

The Christian faith makes guilty sinners into incandescent saints. And it's all supernatural. The essence of Christianity is not behave but behold. Jesus doesn't say, "Perform, earn your righteousness and pay" but simply "Receive abundance of Grace and *My* free gift of righteousness" (Romans 5:17). Where every other religion says "Do, do, do", Jesus says "Done, done, done!"

Peter unpacks our royal identity and mission beautifully:

"But you are a chosen people, a royal priesthood, a holy nation, God's special possession, that you may declare the praises of him who called you out of darkness into his wonderful light."

(1 Peter 2:9)

Jesus didn't come to die and rise again for a religious bunch of pew-warming orphans. He gave His life for a royal priesthood of hell-emptying sons and daughters. John Wesley was an ordinary man set on fire by an extraordinary God. Wesley preached 600 sermons in a row and only 6 of them were inside of churches. He rode on average 25 miles per day across the English countryside, preaching in the open air 3 times a day, establishing orphanages, schools and a Methodist church that in the end would change the very character of the world. There is nothing more exciting than Christianity in the power of God and nothing more boring than church without Him. No, Christianity is not dry, exhausting ritual, but the Holy Spirit empowered, light-releasing declaration of the chosen children of the King. Have you heard, really heard, the good news? Drink it down deep and go tell it abroad.

DAY 50
PLAIN SPEECH, PLAIN POWER, PLAIN MESSENGERS

"We live in a culture that has, for centuries now, cultivated the idea that the skeptical person is always smarter than one who believes. You can almost be as stupid as a cabbage as long as you doubt."
Dallas Willard

The world has made an idol of reason, polishing it with perpetual questioning. This has got into the church. However attractive the vulnerability in which it is packaged, doubt is not a virtue in Christian leadership. Faith comes by hearing, chewing and feasting on the word of God and without faith it's impossible to please God! Whatever is not from faith is sin (Romans 14:23).

I am both haunted by and pulled to answer with my very life a question that Jesus once posed: "When the Son of Man comes, will He really find faith on the earth?" (Luke 18:1)

Uncertainty has become odiously trendy in our grey, postmodern, western culture of intellectual idolatry. Thomas did not get a medal from Jesus for his honesty and stubbornness, neither does he appear in the Hebrews 11 hall of fame. Yes, we all have seasons of wrestling with truth. Notwithstanding healthy occasion for vulnerability, this is our moment to peel away from the public platform and earnestly seek the face of God.

The Holy Spirit doesn't endorse woolly talk. He is never political. Apostolic love in the New Testament was never co-dependent, but backboned, brazen and bloody self-sacrifice on behalf of lost people on their way to hell without repentance and faith.

I believe that church leadership in the west needs to throw out all trendy, political, uncertainty and demonstrate plain faith and godly authority! We are not called to be doubting, intellectual analysts heavy on opinion, but simple messengers, who fear God and not man. I'm not that interested in your opinion Mr. church leader, I want to hear the word of God on the matter! In this next season, I believe that favour and anointing is going to come on men and women without guile and with plain speech. Love is pure. The shepherd-less flocks of the world don't need to be pandered to but saved by and led through and out of darkness by a revered company of incandescent men and women who know their God and hold aloft the light of His word, come what may.

DAY 51
BURNING LAMPS

*"I set myself on fire and people
come to watch me burn."*

John Wesley

Have you ever put your finger in the tiny flame of a candle and expected to come away gently warmed? Try it! You will discover that, however pretty the shape, you can't "turn down" fire. Fire is fire. Fire burns flesh. It consumes whether you like it or not. The Holy Spirit and fire through the born-again believer (Luke 3:16) is hot at a temperature that will always burn with a compassion for the lost, burn with a zeal for the reward of the cross, burn with a jealousy for the glory of His name and burn with a tenacity and love that will offend the flesh, dead religion and the lukewarm carnality of a people fat on other gods.

Saints, without Jesus we can do nothing of eternal value (John 15:5). The world recognises people after the flesh, achievements, possessions, business cards – in heaven we are known by the candle of our spirit. Jesus called His cousin a "burning and shining lamp." Let's cry out for a fresh outpouring of the fire of the Holy Ghost to possess our lives, whatever the cost.

So, then the world and sometimes the church throws the proverbial bucket of cold water our way? Then Hallelujah! G.K. Chesterton said this: *"Jesus promised His disciples three things. That they would be completely fearless, absurdly happy and in constant trouble."* Burn with His zeal anyway, lay your life down on the altar again. Fire falls on dead offerings. We do well to set the world on fire or go to glory early. We are called for such a time as this – to turn the world upside down.

DAY 52
ETERNAL FOUNDATION

"Don't let obstacles along the road to eternity shake your confidence in God's promise. The Holy Spirit is God's seal that you will arrive."
David Jeremiah

One of the foundational doctrines of the Christian faith is eternal judgement (Hebrews 6:1-3). Remember, you can't have an advanced "foundation", a foundation by definition must come at the start. So eternal judgement is entry level doctrine, Christianity 101, we are to build "our house" on it. Why? Well, the world operates by "nowism", the excessive focus on the present, or on immediate gratification. Christianity takes us beyond this world, beyond time and into eternity. And not only that but into God's eternal justice system and His reward system.

To what extent do you live for "the now" or for eternity?

Many Christians hardly have any vision of eternity. They think and act as if everything that matters is going to happen in time. I have struggled with this issue – it's understandable because time, to an extent, is where we are physically stuck. But it is tragic how many people's faiths have been shipwrecked by temporal setbacks and injustices. This often arises from a failure to grasp the importance and reality of eternal judgement (God's fulfillment and reward beyond this life). God sees all. He will set every record straight. This is wonderful news and leads us into deep rest, freedom, joy and hope.

The apostle Paul said this: *"If we who are [abiding] in Christ have hoped only in this life [and this is all there is], then we are of all people most miserable and to be pitied"* (1 Corinthians 15:19). In other words, if you do not have a vision which takes you beyond time and into eternity your condition is pitiable. You will suffer very many disappointments and seeming injustices in this life because time, this span of several decades, is not the fulfillment.

This is precisely why Jesus can afford so adamantly to encourage His disciples to "Be glad and exceedingly joyful" in times of reviling and persecution for righteousness' sake, for our *"reward in heaven is great [absolutely inexhaustible]"* (Matthew 5:10-11). If persecution and rejection is our lot with nothing else added then, again, the Christian should be the pitiful laughing stock, certainly not the rejoicing ones. But if eternity matters as much as Jesus Himself (the great "I AM") knows and says it does, then rejoicing in what is surely coming our way is entirely fitting.

Heaven has a different way of measuring success than the world. The world looks at the "outside of the cup", the superficial, whereas God looks at the heart. There are only three questions we need to ask ourselves regularly with regard to "success":

- *Am I trusting God? (Hebrews 11:6, John 6:29)*

- *Am I doing my best to be faithful with what God has called me to do? (Matthew 25:21)*

- *Am I walking in love? (1 Corinthians 13)*

Friends, be encouraged, this life is only the dressing room for the main stage. The fulfillment comes in eternity. Lay the foundation of eternal judgement in your faith. Build your entire walk on it. Your wisdom will be justified in due time. Our reward will be endless. Your hope in this life, impregnable.

DAY 53
OUR TIMES

"Perhaps He is sleeping in the boat, but He is there. He is always there. He is all-powerful; nothing escapes His vigilance. He watches over each one of us 'as over the apple of His eye.' He is all love, all tenderness."

Fr. Jean C. J. D'Elbee

Grace understands that "our times are in His hands" (Psalm 31:14-15). That's the best place for them. We can take our hands off trying to control and manipulate things, people, events and enter rest. As children of God, we do not earn blessing, we receive it. Sons get an inheritance, not a paycheck. The world promotes self-help – you are the captain of your destiny. As such, there is jealousy, bitterness, anxiety, pride and burn-out.

The kingdom is upside down. We do not strive independently like the orphan, but we trust and enter into what our good Father is doing in us and for us. We take on the easy yoke of Jesus and find rest for our souls. We receive our destiny, our inheritance, as sheer gift, by faith. Scandalous!

Children of God are very irritating to those under the grip of the religious spirit, both in the church or outside of it. Things happen for them that they don't deserve. And that's the point. It's a posture of humility and trust, that shuns any form of "earning mentality" (also known as self-righteousness) by which we actually frustrate the grace of God. A proper understanding of grace, unmerited favour, enables us to enter rest.

Be still and know that He is God (Psalm 46:10). Our times are in His hands, not our own. God is good. Instead of the exhausting white-knuckled grip of manipulation, adopt the open palm of meekness. "Blessed are the meek, for they shall inherit . . ."

Instead of worry, the fight to stay in control, enter into trust, rest, lightness and joy. Instead of regretting the past and living in the future, receive the peaceful and spacious place of enjoying today. Instead of earning, inherit. Take your place as a son and heir by trusting your Father and renouncing all "independence" idolatry. You will end up child-like – thankful, joyful and servant-hearted. Losing your life, only to find it. Happy to be last, you will end up first.

DAY 54
CIRCUMSTANTIAL SUCCESS

*"This is the work (service) that God asks of
you: that you believe in the One Whom He
has sent [that you cleave to, trust, rely on,
and have faith in His Messenger]."*
Jesus (John 6:29)

Defeat the influence of circumstance. Trust in what God is doing in you, not through you. His ways are higher. My work for God is simply to trust Him.

Success in God's eyes isn't a great achievement for God. It's a consistent state of believing and trusting in Jesus.

Steve Backlund said, *"Success isn't a place to reach, but a state of being. We get successful on the inside when we are not successful on the outside. That's the pathway to great leadership."* Great leaders emerge from having great perspectives, not great circumstances. The most influential person in the room is the man with the greatest hope.

"Man is not the creature of circumstances, circumstances are the creatures of men. We are free agents, and man is more powerful than matter." (Benjamin Disraeli)

"As man thinks in his heart so is he." (Solomon)

"Chew on praiseworthy and lovely things . . . and the God of peace will be with you." (Saint Paul)

"The secret is Christ in me, not me in a different set of circumstances." (Elisabeth Elliot)

Where are your eyes fixed today? What you focus on magnifies. Upon what or whom is your chief desire? *"Seek ye first . . ."* (Matthew 6:33). When I make my foremost desire and appetite the reality of Christ, His kingdom and righteousness, I find that His love, joy and peaceful ecstasies swallow up every circumstantial shadow and order every necessary provision (*". . . all these things shall be added unto you."*)

When Jesus has His rightful place in my heart, all other names take their rightful place. When I have made Jesus first love, Lord and Master, and make no mistake that's a decision, losing (even hating) my very life, then I find my real (heavenly) life. Circumstance has then become my servant. Greater is the glorious reality of He within me, than all without!

If trust is success then my trust in God is most evidenced by my thanksgiving- this simple, humble, atomic bomb in the spirit. "In everything give thanks . . ." (1 Thessalonians 5:18) The heavenly aroma of thanksgiving and praise in the midst of suffering and trial shakes the heavens with the result that either the circumstance changes supernaturally or my attitude to it. Both are miracles and either way I am gloriously free. "And the things of earth will grow strangely dim, In the light of His glory and grace . . ."

DAY 55
AN INTEGRATED LIFE

*"If you are faithful in little things, you will
be faithful in large ones. But if you are
dishonest in little things, you won't be
honest with greater responsibilities."*
Luke 16:10 (NLT)

When we make a mess in the natural we tend to clear it up. If I spill milk all over your kitchen, tread mud up the stairs, I clear it up. If I break your china vase I clear it up and probably offer to buy you a new one. How are we faring in the spirit?

Integrity is the knitting together of our entire lives. There is no dualism in the Kingdom of God, no sacred/secular divide – all life is worship. And the spirit realm never sleeps. As Jesus points out, how we fare in the little things is what will come out in the times of greater responsibility.

"Integrity is not something you show others. It is how you behave behind their back. Integrity is choosing courage over comfort; choosing what is right over what is fun, fast, or easy; and choosing to practice our values rather than simply professing them. Integrity is choosing your thoughts and actions based on values rather than personal gain. Wisdom is knowing the right path to take. Integrity is taking it." – Anonymous

If I fail to keep my word, does that matter to me – do I apologize? How much do I even value my commitment, my "Yes" or "No" under heaven? If I have an outburst, do I recognise that fact and clear up my mess? For surely the spiritual filth has been pasted all over the walls, someone else's walls. Or do I tend to go about making bad smells, oblivious to mess and chaos in my slipstream? Can I recognise the injury, transgression and debt both to God, man and myself? And so make recompense, restore trust, rebuild intimacy? These are the things that unless we are sensitive in the spirit, worshipful, hardness of heart creeps in. We can become desensitized to the Lord and to each other, living lives lacking integrity.

One part of holiness is shortening the gap between sin and repentance, prodigal distance and restored intimacy. Thinking clearly, seeing clearly again. Lord, grant us soft hearts, grace, humility and courage to face our mistakes, own our sin and to come to the cross quickly. Awaken us to the atmosphere we carry, that we might clear up our mess and re-clothe ourselves in Your righteousness and fragrance. For Your glory.

"Behold, you desire truth in the inward parts,
And in the hidden part you will make me to know wisdom."
Psalm 51:6

DAY 56
OBEDIENCE IS BETTER

"What God says is best, is best, though all
the men in the world are against it."
John Bunyan, *The Pilgrims Progress*

We will never fully obey God. But the good news (the gospel) is that Jesus has done that already. We are let off the hook by faith in the finished work of the cross. We are completely justified by faith ("holy, blameless, without reproach" assures the scripture), the very righteousness of God, in Christ. That's very relaxing news. Now we get to move out in obedience, not so that we may earn God's love but because we are loved. We can follow Jesus from a place of rest and excitement, rather than resentful, fearful, religious obligation – knowing that God is trustworthy and that He knows what's best for us and how to lead things.

The following is perhaps my favorite scripture on obedience:

"Jesus answered and said to them, 'Most assuredly, I say to you, the Son can do nothing of Himself, but what He sees the Father do; for whatever He does, the Son also does in like manner. For the Father loves the Son, and shows Him all things that He Himself does; and He will show Him greater works than these, that you may marvel."

(John 5:19-20)

There are three things that underpin healthy obedience.

First, we must believe that we are greatly loved by God and designed by Him for a purpose (Psalm 100). The foundation of obedience is love; God's love for us and then ours back towards Him. The posture of trust necessary to fuel our obedience works through love. As Jesus says above, we are built for relationship and collaboration with our Father, not an orphan-hearted, independent view of life. It's our Father's joy to show us our part in His-story, the son's delight to trust and follow. God made us for relationship. He knows, often against our better judgment, that doing life alone is no fun and that, ultimately, it's exhausting, vain and fearful. As we learn to accept our powerlessness and the mutual love and devotion between Father and son, obedience becomes a joy, a delight (Psalm 119:35), rooted in trust and producing lasting fruit, which in time we shall marvel at.

Second, we must repent (change our thinking) and understand that we can do nothing of eternal value without God (John 15:5). This truth is extremely counter-cultural. The definition of "profane" is anything man is doing that God did not initiate. Unless the Lord builds the house the laborers labor in vain.

Third, obedience leads to a life of grace, rest, marvel and wonder. The pressure is off us and on Him. With all of the above in place, we will avoid the pitfalls of vain and exhausting independence and enjoy life in all its abundance. It's unbelief and disobedience that leads to burn out and mediocrity.

In conclusion, arguably the greatest hindrance to obedience, perhaps ironically, is our religious bent – our lust to perform our way into God or man's good books. However, the foolishness of obedience to the call of God is wiser than the greatest wisdom the world has to offer. The next revival or world-changing reformation will come through many whom the world, even parts of the church, regard as complete fools. His wisdom will always confound the worldly wise because His ways are higher. Remember the words of Samuel – "Obedience is better than (the) sacrifice (of religion)."

(Meditate on John 15)

DAY 57
THE NEED TO BE RIGHT

"Another thing that distracts us is our passion for vindication. St. Augustine prayed, "O Lord, deliver me from this lust of always vindicating myself." Such a need for constant vindication destroys our soul's faith in God. Don't say, "I must explain myself," or, "I must get people to understand." Our Lord never explained anything – He left the misunderstandings or misconceptions of others to correct themselves.

When we discern that other people are not growing spiritually and allow that discernment to turn to criticism, we block our fellowship with God. God never gives us discernment so that we may criticize, but that we may intercede."

Oswald Chambers

There is a lie I am slowly letting go of: I have done well and will feel good if I proved someone wrong and "won" an argument (for Jesus). No, I have done well when I have loved someone in the truth. Knowledge puffs up, love edifies. Jesus is far less interested than I in whether I am right or wrong. He looks to see whether I am proud or humble. The kingdom works differently from the world: if I loved not, then I lost. If I was postured in love and humility then I can never lose, never fail. I have realised that when I am rooted in love I listen to others in order to understand. When I am moving out of fear, unsure of who I am at the deepest level, I listen in order to agree.

Community in tension can serve better than resolution with distance. Can I sit comfortably with people whose beliefs are radically different from mine? Or am I insecure, threatened to the core? Do I crave safety through agreement? "There is no fear in love, perfect love casts out fear." (1 John 4:18)

None of us will ever be on the right side of every argument. Neither do we need to be. My need to be right is often the performance fig leaf covering for my shame and fear. When I am offended, first, I am fearful, ashamed, proud. I have forgotten who I really am, a beloved child of God, who has no need of this type of defense, together on a trust-ridden path of mystery and wonder with other beloveds. In any conflict or debate, if I walk in honour with others good fruit will always follow. God resists the proud but grace always comes to the teachable. Let's contend through honour and humility.

DAY 58
A GOOD EYE

"Treat people as if they were what they
ought to be, and you help them become
what they are capable of becoming."
Johann Wolfgang Von Goethe

Jesus said, "The eye is the lamp of the body. If your eyes are healthy, your whole body will be full of light" (Matthew 6:22). What do healthy eyes look like? What did Jesus mean by 'a good eye'? A good eye is a generous disposition, quick to celebrate progress, quick to focus on and believe the best. If someone lacks a good eye, they are stingy in thought, word and deed. Many of us are stingy and critical, with ourselves first and then others.

Do you know we all have a relationship with ourselves? We spend more time with ourselves than any other human being. How do you treat yourself? Do you even like yourself? However we treat ourselves is how we will treat others (Matthew 22:39). If God so loved us in both creating and fashioning us then dying for us, who are we to constantly devalue and criticize ourselves? We are in opposition to the Lamb of God! Ask the Lord to help you love and honor yourself, as He does, and so honor others.

Jesus said, "Do not judge." Paul said, "I don't even judge myself." Having grown up on a diet from the wrong tree (the knowledge of good and evil), this is a lesson I am learning very slowly. But here lies the power of the lamp of seeing, both to receive light and to sculpt with it. The Pharisee has the eye of criticism and offense. Little light can enter. This eye will disempower people and can thwart destiny in those around them.

Whereas God is not critical; God is light and light floods from His face. Honor is the "good eye" of the Father. This "eye" is a perpetual open tap of glory, both ways. When you honor yourself (and quit criticizing yourself), you will honor people and receive Christ's gift in them. You will see them for who they are in the spirit and with that "good eye" you will call them into who they are yet to be.

Love believes the best. Because love focuses on the best. The Father knows who He created, knows the glory hidden in each of us. Creative people (like God) see from a posture of wealth and opportunity. Broken and hurt people see through the murky lens of poverty and lack.

The Father sees people at the end of the race. There might be a need for correction, but the eyes of Jesus never condemn, they always prophetically call us into life's fullness. Remember how the Father viewed His lost son (Luke 15)? He carried a posture of honor and grace. Living with criticism towards ourselves and others is exhausting and dark. Life flows through honor. As you honor your fellow man, believers and unbelievers alike, you will receive the God-given grace on their life. Posture your heart to honor the Lord's grace in those in your environment, not loudly through charm and flattery but with integrity, silently in your heart, and watch your vats begin to overflow with life continually.

Bill Johnson once wrote: *"Religion celebrates perfection. God celebrates progress."*

DAY 59
REMEMBER

"Do this in remembrance of me."
Luke 22:19

I am so forgetful. Sin is paradise lost and then paradise forgotten. Sin is forgetfulness. I forgot who I am. I forgot whose I am. I forgot where I am from. I forgot where I am headed. Remain mindful. Love is patient. Maturity lengthens the gap between stimulus and response. When you are attacked, bend down to the ground and drag a finger in the sand. Engage the Spirit within you and commune with His smiling thoughts. Remember you are the beloved. Remember whose you are. Remember that you are not created to control circumstances or people but to trust and love. Remember who the person in front of you with the stone really is. Even as they have forgotten. Begin to see them at the end of their race and so set the two of you free.

DAY 60
JOYFUL CHILDREN

"Joy is the serious business of Heaven."

C.S. Lewis

Joy is for the childlike. Children trust, they don't have to figure everything out. Orphans (the "world's" adults) need control, with anxiety and restlessness coming as the bad fruit. To laugh I have to let something go. To walk in joy, I have to get comfortable with the tension of unresolved circumstances. Trusting God is essential – walking by faith and not by sight.

I cannot control my circumstances. The only thing or person I can control, on a good day, is myself. There is one who holds everything. We can trust that He is working behind the scenes. We can continually put our lives back in His hands, the only safe place for them.

"He who finds his life will lose it, and he who loses his life for My sake will find it."

Jesus (Matthew 10:39)

Rejoice! Often joy is the fruit of rejoicing before we feel joyful. We don't need joy at the end of the battle, we need joy in the midst of unresolved circumstances. Thanksgiving is a major key. Thanksgiving at all times and for all people, and rejoicing before we get the victory is a display of violent trust, sweet-smelling humility and true worship to our Father. Peace beyond understanding and the joy of abiding in the centre of His presence is then our portion. Bill Johnson said it so well: "If you want to have peace that passes understanding, you have to give up your right to understand everything."

DAY 61
PROSPERITY WITH PURPOSE

*"When God only provides your needs the earth is
lacking the revelation of an abundant father."*
Bill Johnson

If you won the lottery and a briefcase of $20,000,000 was presented to you, you would see something different in your heart from everyone else reading this. Some people would imagine a whole heap of good things, others would imagine some pretty grotesque things, others perhaps a mix. Money is not evil. Money is not the root of all evil. Money is neutral in and of itself.

Money is a great servant, a terrible master. Money is an amplifier or exaggerator of what is in your heart, for good or evil. For this reason, the scripture is true when it says that "the love of money can be the root of all kinds of evil" (1 Tim 6:10) because of what money represents for so many of us. It amplifies the sin in our hearts: the lust for possessions, power, vanity, the endless greed and covetousness it can feed. Alternatively, money can act as a ballast or false god to our insecurity or craving to live independently from God. Our fallen Adamic nature craves control over trust.

For this reason, the love of God using money can also be the root of all kinds of righteousness. If your heart is consecrated and pure, in submission to the word and will of the Father, money will amplify and empower those beautiful seeds – giving, saving, funding international missions, charity enterprise, training, empowering and feeding the poor, housing the orphans, building schools, hospitals and righteous businesses. What's your dream?

The church needs to come out of the dark ages regarding her view of money. Yes, the subject has been abused, like any topic that has tremendous potential for good. Let's not throw the baby out with the dirty bath water. The word "prosperity" has become a curse word amongst many church streams. There is nothing holy about being poor. There is nothing holy about being rich. My level of financial wealth is not an indication of my spiritual maturity, unless it is (Luke 19:24) In both instances, our hearts reveal our level of consecration, not our bank statements.

In truth, poverty and lack is a curse, for neither exist in heaven. "On earth as it is in heaven" is one of the most famous prayers ever uttered, by God Himself. God created and likes nice things! He is very happy for His children to own beautiful things as long as they don't own His children. It always comes back to the heart and a good Father wanting us to live free. God looks at the heart, man looks at the surface.

The false piety message that has been built around shunning wealth and staying poor can be an excuse to relinquish our responsibility to steward the little we are given well so that we can be trusted with entire cities (Luke 19:17). It takes greater faithfulness to steward much, than to bury little. The Lord takes this very seriously. (Luke 19:11-27) Can the Father trust us so that He might prosper us for Kingdom purpose? The Bible says that the wealth of the wicked is coming to the church. But will we have a track record in righteous stewardship? Let's learn to stop fearing money, to quit buying into the religious lies and learn to steward money and cherish it as a tutor for maturity in our own hearts, commissioning each dollar or pound as a soldier for abundant good in the lives of others.

DAY 62
A BEAUTIFUL MIND

*"Do not be conformed to this world (this age), [fashioned
after and adapted to its external, superficial customs],
but be transformed (changed) by the [entire] renewal of
your mind [by its new ideals and its new attitude] . . ."*
Romans 12:2

Take your thoughts captive or they will take you captive.

Research indicates that as much as 75% percent of everything
we think is negative, counterproductive and works against us.
(*A Better Way to Think*, Norman Wright)

Dr Caroline Leaf said this: "75% to 95% of the illnesses that
plague us today are a direct result of our thought life. What
we think about affects us physically and emotionally. It's an
epidemic of toxic emotions. The average person has over 30,000
thoughts a day. Through an uncontrolled thought life, we create
the conditions for illness; we make ourselves sick! Research
shows that fear, all on its own, triggers more than 1,400 known
physical and chemical responses and activates more than 30
different hormones. There are INTELLECTUAL and MEDICAL
reasons to FORGIVE! Consciously control your thought life and
start to detox your brain."

It was Sigmund Freud who promulgated the belief that the
cause of depression "was anger turned on the self." However,
it was Aaron Beck, a disciple of Freud, who, in 1963, concluded
that depressed people were depressed because they "exhibited
a systematic distortive pattern in their thinking processes." In other
words, people succumb to depression because of their systematic
pattern of negative twisted thinking. (ibid. Paul R. Chipman)

Watch out for "The Filthy Five"

1. *Regrets of the Past*
2. *Fear of the Future*
3. *Unhealthy Comparisons*
4. *Self-condemning thoughts*
5. *Temptation*

Modern science yet again backs up what Jesus and the Bible has been saying all along: "Repent". Change your thinking. Wash out your belief system in order to enter into fullness of life.

> *"For though we walk (live) in the flesh, we are not carrying on our warfare according to the flesh and using mere human weapons. For the weapons of our warfare are not physical [weapons of flesh and blood], but they are mighty before God for the overthrow and destruction of strongholds, [Inasmuch as we] refute arguments and theories and reasonings and every proud and lofty thing that sets itself up against the [true] knowledge of God; and we lead every thought and purpose away captive into the obedience of Christ"* (the Messiah, the Anointed One).
>
> (2 Corinthians 10:3-5)

Friends, what we focus on, we connect with in the spirit and it grows, and what we agree with, we empower.

Bill Johnson said this, *"The mind is either at war with God or it is being renewed. There is no middle ground."* He continues, *"The renewed mind is sustained repentance – a changed perspective on how reality functions."* The renewal of the mind is intentionally thinking from God's point of view. It involves an active resistance of worldly lies, a refusal to conform to worldly patterns and an inward agreement with the word of God, releasing God to bring transformation in our lives. Today, may walking with truth, Jesus, and abiding in His word, set you gloriously free (John 8:30-32) and in turn bring freedom to those around you. May the world thrive through your beautiful mind.

DAY 63
THANKSGIVING

"Worry does not empty tomorrow of its sorrow.
It empties today of its strength."
Corrie Ten Boom

Interrupt anxiety with gratitude. If you are good at worrying then you are good at meditating. Just change the tape! Be militant in addressing an unbelieving thought life. The world has no problem calling murder or rape sin. But God views anything apart from absolute reliance on Him as sin (Romans 14:23). Why? Because when we are not trusting in God we are leaning on and trusting in an idol, which will curse us. It's the way we are made and the way the spirit realm has been set up.

"Worry is usurping God's authority", writes Bill Johnson. We must learn to hate and renounce our worrying ways. See them for the destructive rebellion and thieving sin that they truly are. John Wesley said that he would no sooner worry than lie or steal. Worrying achieves nothing but it robs peace, joy, love and rest both in our lives and the lives around us.

Worry is a fight to stay in control. It's a form of pride, whereas trust and thanksgiving is rooted in humility; we actively choose to step off the throne and let a good Father, who knows what he is doing, be God.

By trusting God, you will find rest for your soul, whatever the circumstances. Hate sin, renounce worry, and rejoice always! Choose communion unceasing and in everything give thanks. Fill your life daily with the word of God, which will bring faith (Romans 10:17). Be filled endlessly with the powerful presence of His Holy Spirit – this will energize your faith. Your tongue will then line up with truth and steer your steps into ever increasing life. Your words will create worlds. Worry and anxiety will steadily become a thing of the past. You will impart faith and victory everywhere you go.

DAY 64
THANKSGIVING FOR ALL MEN

"Therefore I exhort first of all that
supplications, prayers, intercessions, and
giving of thanks be made for all men."
(1 Timothy 2:1)

This is a huge scripture. There are no exceptions here, no people whom the Lord does not wish us to pray for, intercede for and give thanks for. The scripture goes on to talk about those in authority particularly. It was an exhortation given to Timothy by Paul the apostle in the midst of governmental persecution. This scripture is just as much for our benefit as it is for the people we are called to pray for.

Honestly, I find this extremely hard to obey, but I am getting there. It flies in the face of my carnal instinct. Well isn't that the gospel! In the midst of a dark world, with evil decisions made at the highest level, why should we give thanks for all men?

Sure, it's a joy to thank God for the righteous, those whom inspire us unto godliness. But why give thanks for the unrighteous? Remember, we are never giving thanks for evil, but we give thanks for the person because of the next three verses and something Paul touches on in chapter 4: ". . . that we may lead a quiet and peaceable life in all godliness and reverence. For this is good and acceptable in the sight of God our Savior, who desires all men to be saved and to come to the knowledge of the truth." (1 Timothy 1:3-4)

First, thanksgiving sets something or someone apart unto God. Later on in the same epistle Paul writes, "For every creature of God is good, and nothing is to be refused if it is received with thanksgiving; for it is sanctified by the word of God and prayer." (1 Timothy 4:4-5) There is no partiality with God and thanksgiving sanctifies and sets apart. Thanksgiving meekly places someone in God's hands and out of ours (freeing us from our controlling propensity) and that's the best place for anything or anyone.

Second, the giving of thanks is the quickest way for each of us to walk in the peace of God. We enter His gates wearing that reverential, grateful, trusting, humble posture. Thanksgiving is the enemy of pride, unforgiveness, resentment, bitterness, strife, contention, comparison, jealousy, envy and finally, perhaps the most dangerous- offence. But the list of dark inheritance in the absence of thanksgiving (Romans 1:21) surely goes on.

Third, thanksgiving is right focus. Can we honour someone for who they are, without stumbling over who they are not? This is the grace of God in Christ Jesus (Romans 5:8). Every person is made in the image of God and God desires that all men (this includes women) be saved and come to the knowledge of the truth, irrespective of the decisions they are making in any given moment. Thanksgiving is about apprehending a divine, gracious perspective, which transcends our knowing and seeing "in part." God loves each person, created them fearfully and wonderfully, knows everything about them, and Jesus died for them. So we give thanks for them in order to walk in heaven's eternal, prophetic perspective, ushering God's purposes into the earth as we do so.

Is there a place for rebuke, correction, righteous anger? Absolutely (2 Timothy 3:16). The scripture reads, "Be angry and sin not". In my opinion, the "sinning not" is ensured by our love-fuelled intercessions and giving of thanks for people in the midst of any conflict- it ensures our hearts are kept pure and soft as we speak truth in love (Ephesians 4:15). It ensures we are walking in perpetual grace, mercy, forgiveness and freedom. If there is anyone we cannot give thanks for, we are bound (Matthew 18:21-35). Thanksgiving sets us free! This is something I am learning slowly, sometimes painfully, but surely. Here, we really need the fear of God, the beginning of wisdom.

Why not take a few people in high office, or any close to you, particularly those whom you strongly disagree with, or those even who have betrayed you, and ask for God's heart for them today? Forgive, pray and give thanks for them. This is Christlikeness. "Father, forgive them, for they know not what they do . . ."

TELL THE TRUTH

*"In a time of deceit telling the
truth is a revolutionary act."*

George Orwell

We live in a world where popularity is a very strong currency. Instagram likes, YouTube views, trending, hashtags. We are reminded at almost every turn in our screen saturated, social media world of interaction, who likes and appreciates what and who seemingly doesn't. If we are not careful, we can easily allow what is popular (or not) to define what is valuable, more importantly, true.

Jesus made some astonishing comments on truth. Here are a few. First, that He is truth. That's bold. Second, that His word is truth (which follows). Third, that only the truth sets free. Stunning. Fourth, that there is a very real devil who lies, is the Father of every lie and that his lies lead to bondage, robbery and destruction in our lives. Finally, Jesus also made it very clear by His teaching and His life and death that truth is rarely popular. There are countless verses (and heroic stories) in the scriptures on the reward of persecution for the faithful.

"There's trouble ahead when you live only for the approval of others, saying what flatters them, doing what indulges them. Popularity contests are not truth contests – look how many scoundrel preachers were approved by your ancestors! Your task is to be true, not popular."

Jesus (Luke 6:26)

Having established Himself as the way, the gate and the truth, perhaps Jesus' most telling and sobering comment on truth, the masses, popularity and salvation comes in His famous sermon on the mount –

"Enter by the narrow gate; for wide is the gate and broad is the way that leads to destruction, and there are many who go in by it. Because narrow is the gate and difficult is the way which leads to life, and there are few who find it."

(Matthew 7:13-14)

Broad and easy is the way to destruction, with many choosing it. Narrow and difficult is the path of life, with "few" choosing it. I hardly know what do with this earth-shattering sentence from the Lord. Can the very ministry of God yield only "few"?

What is the point I am trying to make today?

The good news is that the pressure is off us, the church, to save the world. This generation of lost souls is not our responsibility. Our only responsibility is to gladly and joyfully walk in obedience, truth and love, to preach the gospel and let God the Spirit deal with the hearts of sinners. God will not rate us on our numbers. Jeremiah's ministry was a disaster in that regard. Furthermore, we must never rate the validity of "our ministry" by the number of likes we garner on Facebook or the size of our audience in any given arena.

Importantly, this should not dissuade us from hoping, praying and sacrificing for the multitudes of lost to come home. Jesus tells a story of 99 sheep "safe" and only one lost sheep to be found, which the good shepherd will go after (Luke 15). In other words, Jesus desires all to come home to the Father. This too must be our desire and mission. But it should ensure that our emphasis remain fixed on glorifying God alone in the process, come what may.

In any case, ensuring that our ministry is unto God first and then people is the only way we can love people well. If people want Jesus (the biblical Jesus), if they want salvation (the biblical way), that is between them and God. It is absolutely not for us to manipulate truth into lies so that we can feel better about the life we have chosen, the ministry we are walking in, the popularity with men and the "success" we think we are walking in.

We must live for an audience of One. This is freedom. Jesus regularly offended people. Jesus had "non-Christians" walk away in dismay and He didn't chase them down or try to make them feel better or the situation easier (Mark 10:21-23). Jesus also had "many" disciples walk out on Him and He didn't placate their grumbling, offence or unbelief either (John 6:60-66).

Be encouraged, sometimes it is only the word or action which really slays, following which you will see no apparent fruit at the time (perhaps the very opposite), which years later will have produced a whole harvest of righteousness in a person or people group's life (John 12:24). Don't be so quick to rate your effectiveness, put your ministry and the people whom you minister to in the hands of God. I love how Robert Louis Stevenson put it- "Don't judge each day by the harvest you reap but by the seeds that you plant."

DAY 66
LOVE NOT THE WORLD
PART 1

"This world is not my home
I'm just a-passing through
My treasures are laid up
Somewhere beyond the blue."

Jim Reeves

I want to hit the famous topic of being in the world but not of the world. For God so loved us all that He gave Jesus to die on a cross to overcome the world and save us out of it, that whoever would believe in Him would not perish but have everlasting life.

Atheists and agnostics often say to me, "Dom, get with the times." It's like I produce a foul stench with my "archaic" beliefs and what I will stand up for. I am so foreign to those people swept up in the tide of today's progressive world-view. Thank God, I say! I have no desire to be "with the times" but with the timeless One. Please understand, I don't aim to be foreign by sporting dodgy sandals and keeping an unkempt beard (although, ironically, this is now cool again . . . I think?), I aim to be faithful to the Lord and His truths, which I have chosen to submit to. We all bow somewhere. I am called to be down in the nitty gritty of the world but bowing at a throne altogether apart from it.

Listen to what Jesus says about the born-again believer's condition with regards to the world. *"Because you are not of the world, but I chose you out of the world, therefore the world hates you."* (John 15, circa 33AD). "Therefore". I have cited the approximate date because I want us to notice something about time with regards to the "world".

It is impossible for the one hosting the Holy Spirit of God to be loved by the "world". Ever. If you open your mouth faithfully you will garner hatred. 'Or do you think that the Scripture says in vain, *"The Spirit who dwells in us yearns jealously?"* (James 4:5). So, in this context, what is "the world"? Scripture tell us: *"For all that is in the world – the lust of the flesh, the lust of the eyes, and the pride of life – is not of the Father but is of the world."* (1 John 2:16). J.C. Ryle (1816-1900) wrote, *"Laughter, ridicule, opposition and persecution are often the only reward which Christ's followers get from the world."*

John Wesley preached 100 years earlier than Ryle and is, to this day, named (rather ironically) as the greatest Oxford Alumni in their history. Oh how we love to build the tombs of the prophets that our fathers killed (Luke 11:47-51). Early Methodism turned the world upside down for Jesus. But, at the time, Wesley had pieces of dead cat thrown at him whilst he preached and mobs regularly tried to burn down the houses that he slept in. In the past years, three of my best friends from school have called me an out of date bigot, a fascist . . . like Hitler. I was forced to leave a dinner party when I spoke up about the bible's stance on sexual sin. Kindergarten persecution, granted. But it's going to get worse and more glorious, so let's be prepared.

DAY 67
LOVE NOT THE WORLD
PART 2

"But our citizenship is in heaven. And we eagerly await a Saviour from there, the Lord Jesus Christ."
Philippians 3:20

What we need to understand, really get, is that the "world" is under the power of the devil (1 John 5:19). It always will be until Christ's return. That's biblical. It's a major theme in the New Testament. It's very obvious when you take a cursory glance at the news today and church history. This thing, this battle we're in, isn't about 21st century progressivism, or "getting with the times". It's about the world, the harlot Babylon (Revelation 16:19) vs. the bride Jerusalem, "the holy city" (Revelation 21:2,10). It's about righteousness vs. evil, light vs darkness – just with a new, savvy, ear-tickling marketing spin. It's the spirit of the world, the antichrist spirit vs. those saved out of it and filled with the Holy Spirit. People dead in sin or dead to sin.

The world cannot "progress". It's run by the devil and under judgement (Romans 3:19, John 12:31). The world with its systems, spiritual principalities and powers, is a dead end. Get out, today if necessary. Each man is either dead to the world, by being born again through crucifixion with Christ and water baptism burial or they are going down with it. That's why Jesus says, *"You must be born again to enter the kingdom of God."* There's no other type of Christian.

If your Christianity offends nobody, requires no sacrifice – then it costs nothing, and is worth nothing. Persecution from the world is evidence that you no longer belong to it – that you're not in bed with it (James 4:4). So, put bluntly, if you aren't persecuted, then you need to question where you really belong and from which altar your words (or lack of them) evidence your worship. Whoever wants to be a friend of the world makes himself an enemy of God.

Charles Spurgeon said this: *"That very church which the world likes best is sure to be that which God abhors."*

I realize these are strong words but there is a war going on for your soul and your devotion. Parts of the church are going into deep deception right now because the pressure to conform is too great. This life is short. I love people too much to stay silent and to compromise your eternity over my comfort. Love the people in the world by hating the spirit of the world and being dead to it. People can smell a life that is truly free and many will one day thank you that you broke free of the miserable altar which they are chained to, that you ceased operating on the putrid (spiritual) trading floor upon which they carry out their daily dealings. Our worship, our separation is loud, even when we are silent. Be encouraged, saints, no servant is above his Master. Our love costs, but reward is coming. Your wisdom will be justified.

DAY 68
DISTURBANCE AND GROANING

"No man's life is greater than his prayer life."
Leonard Ravenhill

There is much cause for celebration, hope and joy in the gospel of grace. There is also heady fuel for sober intercession and urgent mission.

When the church side-lines the uncomfortable doctrines of hell, God's wrath and Judgement Day, we make a vanity of the cross. It is a deep arrogance, masquerading as compassion, that says we know and love better than God by excluding these uncomfortable topics from our teaching, preaching and conversation. Either the death and resurrection of Jesus is an ultimatum for every human soul or the Father is cruel for letting not that terrible cup pass Jesus by at Gethsemane. The Lamb slain must not merely dress the lyrics of our hymn sheets, stain the glass windows of our buildings nor delicately litter our inoffensive relations – it must disturb, disrupt, compel and set ablaze.

What consumes you? Something will consume you, you can be sure of that. Every life is an altar. The question is to what or whom are you given? Who is Master? You cannot serve two. I will burn with the lusts and trivialities of the flesh or the yearnings of the Bridegroom. I am a friend of the world or a friend of God, never both. Every person is given to intimacy with the world or bridal devotion to God. We each decide. That's our awesome privilege. We are fools, slaves, lovers to our chosen god or God. The universe is headed for a Great Wedding. Have you answered the invitation? Is the Bride dressed correctly? Is she beautifying herself? Let holy fire fall on the sacrifice of your life today and set the world ablaze. The earth is groaning like a woman in labour for your manifest sonship.

DAY 69
JOHN'S BAPTISM

*"Today the whole world is under the wrath
of God. For one to be baptised today means
he goes through God's wrath. But he does
not only go through it; he comes out of it. His
emergence from it shows that he is the one
who has come out. This is baptism."*

Watchman Nee

Baptism is not a tradition, it's a command, a burial and a resurrection. Jesus commands repent, believe and be baptised (fully immersed) "that you might be saved". In other words, once you have arrived at a conscious decision to make Jesus Lord and Saviour, die with Him, that you might live (eternally) with Him.

The Old Testament is full of 'types' for the New Testament believer in Jesus. Faith saves us, baptism separates us from the world. For example, Noah and the eight were saved in the Ark (Jesus), "through water" (1 Peter 3:20). The Ark was Christ, the flood was God's judgement on the earth. In the Ark we pass through water safely. Outside of the Ark we are destroyed.

Another example: the blood of the Passover lamb on the doorpost saved Israel's firstborn in Egypt and they escaped from Egypt through the deadly waters of the Red sea. Similarly, we are saved only by the blood of Jesus (Lamb of God) and through water baptism from our personal 'Egyptian' slave chains. There's nothing quaint or traditional about baptism imagery. The biblical, prophetic symbolism of New Testament baptism is so majestic, so violent, that if it weren't pregnant with solid hope, it would be terrifying.

Derek Prince (author, *They Shall Expel Demons*) affirms that full immersion water baptism is the only way to keep your deliverance from demonic power. Jesus, the Philippian jailor, the Ethiopian eunuch (Acts 8:38) and all early church believers were baptised by full immersion in water straight away. May it be the same for us today – it's urgent and it's a command.

I'm going to say something controversial. I hope we can stay friends or that you will at least track with me, think deep and pray about this! I believe that sprinkling children at baptism helps sustain carnal, powerless Christianity. Those beautiful little gifts of God never repented, they never believed in the finished work of Calvary, they never died with Christ. So they certainly aren't born again. Unless we dedicate babies to God, pray and prophesy over them (as usual, the life of Jesus is our model), I believe we help Adam live in the church.

Why? In biblical water baptism I am forced to identify with Jesus in His death, burial and resurrection (Romans 6). Indeed, once I have been buried and raised again my life does not belong to me (1 Corinthians 6:19-20) but the Holy Spirit. That's good news! Water baptism is my death sentence, resurrection life eternal in Christ, starting now, empowered by the Holy Spirit is my portion and inheritance.

When we learn to plunge only the new, repentant, believing believer into the watery grave of baptism, we will see resurrection power restored in a church that is no longer owned and overcome by the world but rather overcomes the world and destroys the powers of darkness as the resurrected Christ pulsates through her. Let's stop messing about with pretty white dresses and archaic fonts, placating our Spirit-quenching traditions, and mess up some bathrooms, invade some local rivers, split some Red seas with repentant believers fresh out of the bondage of Egypt!

Many oppose biblical baptism. We must understand that this is a religious stronghold with a nasty demon attached. That wicked spirit, the whole demonic realm knows the power it loses when a repentant believer goes under the waters – all generational iniquity is broken off them. This is a major deal – freedom and power is at stake.

DAY 70
AUDIENCE OF ONE

"The secret of Elijah's praying and the character of the man are found in the words, 'Before whom I stand."
E.M. Bounds

When I am cowardly, it is because I have forgotten before whom I stand. I have become earth-bound, temporal and impressed with the honour that man bestows (John 5:44). One reason parts of the church has become flippant, timid and, at worst, plain heretical with the word of God is because she has forgotten before whom she really stands. The craven-hearted church stands only before men.

Before whom do you stand? Who is your audience, ultimately? Before we can walk in our destiny as disciples, effective with the proclamation of the word of God, we must first tremble at it. Isaiah 66:2: *"But on this one will I look: On him who is poor and of a contrite spirit, And who trembles at My word."* It is for our greatest good that we must have a reverence and fear of the word of God. These are the ones that get God's attention.

In John 12:47-48, Jesus makes an astonishing statement: *"And if anyone hears My words and does not believe, I do not judge him; for I did not come to judge the world but to save the world. He who rejects Me, and does not receive My words, has that which judges him – the word that I have spoken will judge him in the last day."* We are going to stand before almighty God and give account for our lives. Every single one of us. Imagine that. That should make us tremble.

However, the above scripture is saying that, in effect, we are going to stand before the word of God and the word will judge us. So, wisdom is to have the same trembling before the word now. Not a cavalier, consumer-culture, pic 'n' mix, man-pleasing flippancy. Like Elijah, you will only have the boldness to confront darkness and wicked rulers to the extent that you are already standing reverently before the word of God, all other opinion and voice paled into vain insignificance. Stand before the Word now and you will not compromise before men.

DAY 71
DON'T BE AFRAID TO FAIL ... OR SUCCEED

*"You are the light of the world. A town built on
a hill cannot be hidden. Neither do people light
a lamp and put it under a bowl. Instead they put
it on its stand, and it gives light to everyone in
the house. In the same way, let your light shine
before others, that they may see your good
deeds and glorify your Father in heaven."*

Matthew 5:14-16

Shine! Jesus commands you: "Let your light shine before men."
Not your neighbour's . . . your light! And, yes, before men. Don't
hide your light under a dish of false humility. Can you imagine if
flowers didn't blossom because they thought they might offend
their neighbours with their bright colours, elaborate petals and
thick fragrance? Can you imagine if the ostrich didn't walk tall?
Love says there is space for all of us to be the fullest and most
beautiful versions of ourselves. There is room in the garden
for all of us to succeed. Fear says there's not enough to go
around or for everyone to be a massive blessing. So, fear must
control people.

Fear lives small. Fear lives dull and meticulously careful,
under the tyrant of perfectionism where failure is illegal. So, we
rob God and rob our neighbour of who we really are. There is
nothing arrogant about living true to your design. Arrogance is
rooted in fear. The false self must come to the fore to cover our
shame. Arrogance is the counterfeit of true humility – trusting
in your true, God-given expression. Humility is rooted in love,
focused on love and so won't let the false self get in the way of
your truest expression.

Bill Johnson comments – "Don't let those satisfied with lack define your boundaries on the goodness of God." Declare war on the voice that says you are not allowed to be amazing. Don't you dare be defined by other people's insecurities. Only ever be defined by the word of God. You are fearfully and wonderfully made – His masterpiece. Your Father is God. You are built to be incredible. Shine, spark and dazzle! Let truth set you free and your freedom free others.

DAY 72
ADAM OR CHRIST?

"Trials teach us what we are; they dig up the soil,
and let us see what we are made of."

Charles Spurgeon

Take a look at which circumstances manifest Adam in you or Christ in you. Whatever triggers the old nature is usually an indication of how the Lord is dealing with you to bring about greater freedom in your life. Jesus died and rose from death. Why? Not just so you could get into heaven but so that heaven could get into you. Christianity is not about religion, it's about Christ being formed in you.

Jesus didn't die so that you would never have your feelings hurt again, but so that the Holy Spirit in you would govern your soul and shape your feelings. Our feelings matter; Jesus wept and Jesus weeps. But then He is quick to raise the dead. Jesus didn't die so that you would never walk through trial again but so that you would walk above your circumstances and so have contentment at all times.

The Father is far less concerned with what you are achieving or acquiring than with whom you are becoming. It's all about our hearts. Are you becoming love? Christ in you, the hope of glory, is not abstract theology. Instead, it's the pragmatic spirituality of your inwardly glorious reality beginning to manifest in every natural circumstance so that the kingdom of heaven invades, from the inside out, every place your feet tread. As Jesus modelled, you have authority over any storm you can sleep in.

How do you deal with things not going your way? Do you manifest anger and anxiety working through fear and control? Or meekness and peace, working through trust? Is the "self" Lord or is Jesus Lord of your life? Spiritual maturity isn't how well you know the Bible or even whether you are raising people from the dead but whether you have the capacity to be joyful in all circumstances. Don't waste your trials. Let them kindly and graciously tutor you into headier heights of joy, freedom and fruit. Let every pruning season yield the utmost for His highest.

Contentment regardless is better than all the tea in china, wisdom better than gold.

Let go of control and trust in a good God who knows what He's doing in your life. He started this great salvation. He steers it, He will perfect and finish it. We get the beautiful privilege of saying yes please, thank-you and watching Him turn everything wonderfully on its head. By grace, through faith and with patience, we inherit the promises. Hallelujah!

DAY 73
SUFFERING AND REJOICING

*"In the secular view, suffering is never seen as a
meaningful part of life but only as an interruption."*
Tim Keller

Is the suffering in your life an interruption, or will you dare to pick up your cross and let it yield the redemptive purpose He might bring in the crucible of devoted surrender and trust?

"And since we are joined to Christ, we also inherit all that he is and all that he has. We will experience being co-glorified with him provided that we accept his sufferings as our own."

(Romans 8:17)

Suffering is actually at the heart of the Christian faith. But often we are bewildered at its arrival. "Beloved, think it not strange concerning the fiery trial which is to try you . . ." (1 Peter 4:12-14) There is nothing necessarily glamorous about following Jesus. But it is glorious. A New Testament theology of suffering restored to the overly seeker-sensitive Western church will prevent many shipwrecked Christian walks which have little expectation of crashing against the shores of persecution, felt isolation and trial. The Christian has traded all superficial glamour and worldly success for intimate, ecstatic, hidden glory via a daily cross-walk, with suffering, rejoicing and eternal reward.

Tim Keller adds: "Christianity teaches that, contra fatalism, suffering is overwhelming; contra Buddhism, suffering is real; contra karma, suffering is often unfair; but contra secularism, suffering is meaningful. There is a purpose to it, and if faced rightly, it can drive us like a nail deep into the love of God and into more stability and spiritual power than you can imagine . . .

While other worldviews lead us to sit in the midst of life's joys, foreseeing the coming sorrows, Christianity empowers its people to sit in the midst of this world's sorrows, tasting the coming joy." ('Walking with God through Pain and Suffering')

God is always good. Even when we can't fathom what's going on around us, we can trust in His nature. I love how Charles Spurgeon puts it: "God is too good to be unkind and He is too wise to be mistaken. And when we cannot trace His hand, we must trust His heart." In our day may the family of God come closer together to share in Christ's sufferings, with each other and through the joyful lens and sure hope of coming redemption and ever weightier glory.

DAY 74
CHARIOTS OF FIRE

*"Bring me my bow of burning gold, bring me my
arrows of desire, bring me my spear, o clouds
unfold! Bring me my chariot of fire."*
William Blake

No one dissuades me from preaching the gospel more than a certain type of Christian. They would rather I was, well, quieter. This battle is not with them. I am not on this earth to meow to the behest of quietly-desperate-middle-England, anaesthetized by the political spirit and material comfort. I shall roar unto my Saviour in the power of the Holy Spirit and for the sake of His drowning ones. Let everything that has breath praise the Lord!

All the while the devil is possessing men to drive vehicles into God's precious children.

Whom and what are you possessed by? It is something. Be sure to know that preaching Jesus Christ crucified, raised from the dead, from a heart of love and compassion is for Holy Spirit terrorists. The devil doles out fear and death. God's faithful church will terrorise his plans as she doles out faith, hope, love and eternal life in the good news of the cross and resurrection.

CT Studd wrote:

*"Some want to live within the sound of church or chapel bell;
I want to run a rescue shop, within a yard of hell."*

Saints! Today is a gift, not a right. Your life is no longer your own. Get in your chariot of fire. We have a rescue mission of unfathomable importance. The devil is terrified of those whom the Almighty and His angelic guard goes with. Never be silent with the gospel. Never bow to the serpent's delicate persuasions, even if it comes via a "well-meaning" Christian. The Lord commands "Preach." To preach the Lord's glorious gospel, let alone in the context of His proposed "rooftop" (Matthew 10:27), is the absolute antithesis of speechless, lukewarm, watered-down decorum that the spirit of the world or religious traditionalism might ensnare you with. Make some noise for Christ's sake! Shine your light. Your "foolish wisdom" (1 Corinthians 1:18-21) will be justified.

DAY 75
JESUS JUICE

"But the fruit of the [Holy] Spirit [the work which
His presence within accomplishes] is love, joy
(gladness), peace, patience (an even temper,
forbearance), kindness, goodness (benevolence),
faithfulness, Gentleness (meekness, humility),
self-control (self-restraint, continence). Against such
things there is no law [that can bring a charge]."
Galatians 5:22-23 (AMPC)

When you get squeezed what comes out? If you squeeze an apple, you get apple juice. A tree is known by its fruit and the quality therein. It's the same for us. When you get squeezed, what comes out? When Christians get squeezed, Christ should manifest.

When it comes to spiritual maturity, man can be divided into two camps: orphans and sons. Orphans have little or no relationship with the Father of all creation. Sons are reconciled to the Father through Jesus and, through a deep trust in the goodness of His nature, live according to what they see the Father doing. Sons live for His will not their own.

When squeezed, Orphans react and are quickly offended. Orphans are defensive and over-sensitive because they fear. Squeeze a fearful one and fear comes out. Orphans feel alone. It's a generational pattern of iniquity and the discipleship of the world. Orphans manipulate, people-please and engineer their way to the top, because they don't have a loving Father who knows what's best looking out for them.

But a Christian has become a child of God and abides not in fear but in perfect love. This changes everything. Sons don't react in lonely, fearful independence but respond from the hope-saturated communion and protection of a good Father.

The peaceful presence of the Dove is their greatest treasure. Meekness, carnality restrained, has become their place of unlimited inheritance.

Bill Johnson said this: *"When we go through that veil of opposition and live from kingdom response, that's where the promotion comes from."*

Whether we react or respond in trial tells an awful lot about where we are seated. When love is squeezed, love comes out, casting out fear. Jesus – *"When He was reviled and insulted, He did not revile or offer insult in return; [when] He was abused and suffered, He made no threats [of vengeance]; but he trusted [Himself and everything] to Him Who judges fairly."* (1 Peter 2:23 AMPC) This is meekness personified.

When squeezed and poked, do I fight for myself, or do I commit myself? Orphans must judge and fight for themselves. Sons breathe trust, humility and commit themselves and others to perfect Justice. Commit everything unto the Eternal One today, your wisdom will be justified, your peace and joy will be endless.

"And this I pray, that your love may abound still more and more in knowledge and all discernment, that you may approve the things that are excellent, that you may be sincere and without offense till the day of Christ, being filled with the fruits of righteousness which are by Jesus Christ, to the glory and praise of God."

(Philippians 1:9-11)

DAY 76
BE STILL

"I am the vine, you are the branches."
Jesus (John 15:5)

The success of your life depends on one thing. Time in the manifest presence of God. That's it. It's no more complicated. There must be a spiritual violence in each of us after His face. A deep unto deep romance for His whisper, a waterfall of thirst. For there is a myriad of clamorous voices, a plethora of feeding troughs demanding your attention and appetite today.

The posturing, counterfeit justification of busyness and achievement is your enemy, your worry incubator (Luke 10:38-42). Distraction and shallow entertainment is your joy thief. Eugene Peterson said this: *"Prayer is the way we work our way out of the comfortable but cramped world of self and into the spacious world of God."* Be still and know that He is God, none other. Come into rest. Assume your position as a fruitful branch, a grace addict – wonderfully dependent on the happy "sap" of Holy Spirit.

Don't peck the earth like a dirt-scratching chicken, soar like an eagle in the peaceful heights as you simply wait on the Lord. Steal heaven's happy kisses throughout the day. Overflow with glory and spill salvation and Father's purposes wherever you tread.

DAY 77
THE MORTIFICATION OF BUSY

*"Busyness is moral laziness [because it is often a
statement of our self-importance and our excuse
to be inattentive to people] . . . But God has given
us just enough time to do what we need to do
moment by moment to respond to him. And
his grace is there; it is eternally present. Every
moment is a sacrament where time touches
eternity and there is exactly enough time to
do what God has called us to do."*

Bruce Hindmarsh

Busyness and distraction are often manifestations of our poverty
of soul, our craving to cover spiritual nakedness with activity,
our fear of being alone and our inability to live powerfully from
the inside out, as opposed to becoming a victim of outside
demands imposed upon us. Now, I have never been, nor
will ever be, a mother with small children, so I want to tread
carefully on the topic of busyness! However, this is a spiritual
issue, which stems from our heart and motivation and has less
to with our subjective agendas.

Busyness wars against stillness of soul. I'm not advocating a
life of lying about in hammocks – those who abide in Jesus can
be high achievers, as long as they are continually sensitive to the
impulse of the Holy Spirit. Jesus corrected Martha not because
she was serving Him but because she was "anxious and troubled
about many things". Martha had missed the point, the "one
thing" needed to reign in life (Luke 10:38-42)- intimacy with the
Lord first in everything, with our service flowing from that place
of grace. This rested lifestyle takes practice, focus and devotion.
The antidote to busyness is not inactivity or irresponsibility, as

some have accused Mary in the above story, but spiritual rest via remaining present to the Lord at all times.

It helps to ask ourselves the following questions: Am I operating from a place of rest, however long my to-do list is? What is the best way to host a sensitive Dove on my shoulder throughout the day?

Today's world is crowded with information, distraction and shallow entertainment. Multitudes are slaves to the media, suffocating spiritually, heads bowed at their hand-held altars sipping on temporal trivialities or seduced and comatosed by the blazing light pouring forth from a fifty inch face offering pixelated escapism and vicarious living. Can you spot the counterfeit? Entertainment and information are the devil's substitute for joy, revelation and divine destiny. "Less" becomes infinitely more when embraced through faith in the reality of an abundant Kingdom within us, a robe of righteousness enveloping us and the eternal call beckoning us, instead of feared through spiritual blindness and the endless, empty acquisition marketed to us by an orphaned world.

Solitude is then the glory of being alone as we dare to face our barrenness, sit in the discomfort of our incompleteness, expose our arid independence and turn back. Turn back! Redeem the time for the days are evil! (Ephesians 5:16) Shun the mediocre craving of the flesh and the arid frivolities of an information age with their restless reward. Close the door. Turn the device off. Breathe. One thing is needed. Be still (Psalm 46:10). Yield to gratitude, divine detail and wonder. There remain present and know the ecstatic communion you were intricately designed for. Drink deep of this experiential knowledge of God. Still your focus on your Bridegroom King and blaze again.

DAY 78
HEAVEN'S SILENCE

*"When He heard that he was sick, He stayed two
more days in the place where He was."*
John 11:6

How are we to cope with the silence of heaven?

Oswald Chambers wrote this:

*"Has God trusted you with His silence – a silence that has
great meaning? God's silences are actually His answers.
Just think of those days of absolute silence in the home at
Bethany. Is there anything comparable to those days in your
life? Can God trust you like that, or are you still asking Him
for a visible answer? God will give you the very blessings
you ask if you refuse to go any further without them, but His
silence is the sign that He is bringing you into an even more
wonderful understanding of Himself."*

In my limited experience, God's silence is the potting soil of
deepened intimacy. My orphan-hearted lust for control wars
against my childlike trust in a good Father who has a higher,
better plan for my life. By denying my obsession with knowing,
understanding, doing, achieving (with its gentle trappings of
masked self-justification) and controlling, this good Father is
already gently whispering to me, calming my raging sea of anxiety
and independence. His silence invites me into deeper "being",
deeper trust, deeper communion and, ultimately, deeper rest.
Rest is my promised land.

Silence can be painful. Silence is humbling. But He is speaking.
*"In the silence you are speaking, in the quiet I can feel the fire
and it's burning, burning deeply . . ."* (Jason Upton). In the silence,

I am reduced to naked, stark communion. And Communion is glorious. *"He makes me to lie down."* (Psalm 23)

Sometimes His heart and value system seem to shout at me in the silence of apparent unanswered prayer. I learn more in His darkened schoolroom of silence than anywhere else. I'm learning to trust His whisper of nearness and cling to His presence . . . in the silence. Be still my soul and wait. *"So the darkness shall be light, and the stillness the dancing"* (TS Eliot).

DAY 79
DRIVEN BY ETERNITY

"Because what may be known of God is manifest
in them, for God has shown it to them (their
consciences). For since the creation of the world His
invisible attributes are clearly seen, being understood
by the things that are made, even His eternal power
and Godhead, so that they are without excuse."

Romans 1: 19-21

It's amazing how hard we in the West will prepare for career steps in this temporal life. We throw thousands of pounds at training, pore over text books, learn pages of notes off by heart. Tell me, how many verses of scripture do you know about your eternal judgement coming up? We are all in an exam right now – and will be for the rest of our lives on this earth. The evaluation won't be for ten years or 50 years. It will be final and affect your eternity.

Right now, every word we speak, every word we don't speak, every thought of the heart, every action, every sin of commission, every sin of omission, every motivation is being evaluated by an all-knowing, all wise, all-seeing, omniscient, omnipotent, omnibenevolent and omnipresent God. One Day, not far from now, perhaps tomorrow, we will all stand before Him and give account for our lives. Everything hidden will be revealed. Everyone will be there. Every knee will bow, on the earth and under the earth, without exception. We will all be judged by one Man, Christ Jesus, King of Kings and Lord of Lords.

For those who have made Jesus Christ their Lord and Saviour they can approach Judgment Day with confidence (1 John 4). For we are saved by grace through faith. It's the gift of God, not of our self-righteous works, lest any man should boast. Each born-again follower of Christ is washed clean of sin by the blood of

Christ but nevertheless judged by what they have done with their talents, how they have loved and how obedient to the call of God they have been with their lives.

For those who have rejected God's free gift of forgiveness in Christ Jesus, they will stand before Almighty God without an advocate – a fearful thing. They will be judged, punished and told to depart from Him into the everlasting fires of hell. God is holy. He is perfectly just. Mercy has been offered through the cross. It is for us to reject. What was achieved by the Prince of Life at Calvary was and is no small thing. It is finished. Heaven has things settled. The Saviour, Jesus Christ – the way, the truth and the life. The only way to heaven isn't changing.

This life is a gift. Not a right. We are made by God and for God. From Him we came and to Him we shall return. Jesus stands at the door of our hearts and knocks. He will not force His way in. It's His kindness and mercy at the cross, His goodness that appeals for our repentance. But we must let Him in. Are you ready? Have you bowed to Jesus and made Him your personal Lord and Saviour? Is your life driven by temporal things that will come to nothing, or are you living with eternity stamped on your eyeballs?

'There are two kinds of people in the end: those who say to God, "Thy will be done," and those to whom God says, in the end, "Thy will de done."' C.S. Lewis.

DAY 80
UNCTION TO PREACH

"We call it unction. It is this unction which makes the word of God "quick and powerful, and sharper than any two-edged sword, piercing even to the dividing asunder of soul and spirit, and of the joints and marrow, and a discerner of the thoughts and intents of the heart." It is this unction which gives the words of the preacher such point, sharpness, and power, and which creates such friction and stir in many a dead congregation. The same truths have been told in the strictness of the letter, smooth as human oil could make them; but no signs of life, not a pulse throb; all as peaceful as the grave and as dead. The same preacher in the meanwhile receives a baptism of this unction, the divine inflatus is on him, the letter of the Word has been embellished and fired by this mysterious power, and the throbbings of life begin – life which receives or life which resists. The unction pervades and convicts the conscience and breaks the heart.

This divine unction is the feature which separates and distinguishes true gospel preaching from all other methods of presenting the truth, and which creates a wide spiritual chasm between the preacher who has it and the one who has it not. It backs and impregns revealed truth with all the energy of God. Unction is simply putting God in his own word and on his own preachers.

What of unction? It is the indefinable in preaching which makes it preaching. It is that which distinguishes and separates preaching from all mere human addresses. It is the divine in preaching. It makes the preaching sharp to those who need sharpness. It distills as the dew to those who need to he refreshed. It is well described as:

"a two-edged sword
Of heavenly temper keen,
And double were the wounds it made
Wherever it glanced between.
'Twas death to sin; 'twas life
To all who mourned for sin.
It kindled and it silenced strife,
Made war and peace within."

This unction comes to the preacher not in the study but in the closet. It is heaven's distillation in answer to prayer. It is the sweetest exhalation of the Holy Spirit. It impregnates, suffuses, softens, percolates, cuts, and soothes. It carries the Word like dynamite, like salt, like sugar; makes the Word a soother, an arranger, a revealer, a searcher; makes the hearer a culprit or a saint, makes him weep like a child and live like a giant; opens his heart and his purse as gently, yet as strongly as the spring opens the leaves. This unction is not the gift of genius. It is not found in the halls of learning. No eloquence can woo it. No industry can win it. No prelatical hands can confer it. It is the gift of God – the signet set to his own messengers. It is heaven's knighthood given to the chosen true and brave ones who have sought this anointed honor through many an hour of tearful, wrestling prayer.

Earnestness is good and impressive: genius is gifted and great. Thought kindles and inspires, but it takes a diviner endowment, a more powerful energy than earnestness or genius or thought to break the chains of sin, to win estranged and depraved hearts to God, to repair the breaches and restore the Church to her old ways of purity and power. Nothing but this holy unction can do this."

Power Through Prayer, Edward M. Bounds

DAY 81
THE CROSS ALONE

*"Do not go where it is all fine music and
grand talk and beautiful architecture. Go
where the Gospel is preached and go often."*

Charles Spurgeon

Behold Peter before the authorities of his day – "Nor is there salvation in any other, for there is no other name under heaven given among men by which we must be saved." (Acts 4:12) Urgent, intrepid, immovable – salvation not an optional extra, but an imperative. I've been in an uncomfortable number of church services recently with no call to repentance, no warning of judgement and hell, nor focus on the cross and living for eternity. It's been mostly calls to love people in inoffensive ways, not dissimilar to NGOs and secular charities. The most important thing in life is eternity. This short life can't even be compared with the eternal ramifications, both deeply positive and fearfully negative, of the Judgment Day that is coming for all of us.

A gospel that doesn't aggressively confront eternity, heaven and hell, makes a vanity of Jesus' death on the cross. Jesus made it clear that He came to the earth to die and had to die in order to save humanity. "The Lamb of God who takes away the sin of the world." God the Father provided no alternative. Jesus made it clear that He is the only way back to God. If you had seen Him, you had seen God. He backed up both claims with resurrection from the dead.

Charles Spurgeon said this: *"We are not responsible to God for the souls that are saved, but we are responsible for the Gospel that is preached, and for the way in which we preach it."*

There is more joy in heaven over one sinner who repents than ninety-nine righteous who have no need. You do the maths.

The most important message of the church will always be repentance and faith towards God for salvation from sin by the blood of Christ alone. That's why to preach the gospel is Christ's number one commission to His apostles and the first use of the anointing. As noble and important as social justice causes are, we are never to hide the offence and 'foolishness' of the gospel and its proclamation behind good deeds which cannot save a man's soul from hell. We are disobeying God, shunning biblical love for a humanist counterfeit and betraying our perishing neighbour. The church must return to an unflinching message of repentance and Christ crucified.

DAY 82
TRUE DANGER

"We are immortal until our work on earth is done."
George Whitefield

Bill Johnson said, *"The most dangerous life is the life without danger"*. The safest place to be is in the centre of God's will, confessing Christ. It might not be safe from a temporal standpoint, it might even be deeply uncomfortable, even physically and mortally dangerous, but regarding eternity you are being confessed before the Father and the angels.

Take some time to read Matthew 10 a few times. Jesus put things in stark perspective to His disciples (in the knowledge that many of them would be martyred for their faith) – "Whatever I tell you in the dark, speak in the light; and what you hear in the ear, preach on the housetops. And do not fear those who kill the body but cannot kill the soul. But rather fear Him who is able to destroy both soul and body in hell." (Matthew 10:27-28)

Jesus makes it clear that our greatest fear should not even be murder or execution but denial of Christ. And so the most dangerous place to be in my view is standing before the Great White Throne of Judgement with an earthly CV littered with cowardice and disobedience. God forbid we the church have the lost of our nation's blood on our hands! Set us on fire Holy Ghost.

God is sovereign. This is good news. Comprehending the sovereignty of God is what will make the church bold in this hour. Paul the Apostle said, *"But I want you to know, brethren, that the things which happened to me have actually turned out for the furtherance of the gospel, so that it has become evident to the whole palace guard, and to all the rest, that my chains are in Christ; and most of the brethren in the Lord, having become confident by my chains, are much more bold to speak the word without fear."* (Philippians 1:13-14)

Look at the life of Jesus. They tried to throw Him off a cliff at the beginning of His ministry and stone Him but He disappeared in the midst of His murderers on several occasions because it wasn't His time (Luke 4, John 8). Even at the time of Jesus' crucifixion, man didn't kill Him. He laid His own life down and said as much to the one who supposedly had power to end his life (John 19:11). How are you postured before earthly rulers? God is sovereign.

The muzzle of intimidation must come off the mouth of the man-bowing church to preach the full gospel boldly again in the fear of God, come what may. Our cry must become "to live is Christ, to die is but our promotion." I have zeal for social justice causes but parts of the church have begun to sidestep the eternal injustice of souls who are set to be lost in hell for eternity. Bold proclamation of the true gospel, the roar of the Lion within against the injustice of a gospel-lite society is returning to the Body of Christ. SAY AMEN!

DAY 83
COURAGE

*"Courage is contagious. When a brave man takes
a stand, the spines of others are often stiffened."*
Billy Graham

Most people know the victorious story of Daniel and the lions' den (Daniel 6). If we are not careful it can trip lazily off the tongue, often with saccharine, Sunday-school innocence, even cartoon imagery. But at the time this drama in Babylon was far from innocent or jolly. It was an event caked in jealousy, murder and apparent tragedy.

We too easily forget that Daniel did not know the end of his refusal to comply with the betrayal of his colleagues along with the idolatry of Darius and the nation he served. Daniel was preparing for death by being gorged alive by lions. For the sake of the integrity of his daily worship! That's how much Daniel's obedience was worth. How palpably real and precious to you is your secret place, your devotion to the one true God?

You see, the very act of obedience to God that could cost you your job, reputation, friendships, family relationships, indeed your very life, could be the very thing that God uses to turn a fellow employee, friend, family, an idolatrous government, even an entire nation back to Himself. But like so many heroes of faith scattered agonisingly and gloriously throughout the pages of scripture, you won't know until the other side of sacrifice. *"No greater love has man than this that he lay down his life for his friends"* (John 15:13). I must remember this: my cowardice is an act of worship, as is my courage, but each at very different altars. True devotion is purified by fire, integrity is tested by good options and both are realised through courage.

"Take the case of courage. No quality has ever so much addled the brains and tangled the definitions of merely rational sages. Courage is almost a contradiction in terms. It means a strong desire to live taking the form of a readiness to die. 'He that will lose his life, the same shall save it' . . .

He can only get away from death by continually stepping within an inch of it. A soldier surrounded by enemies, if he is to cut his way out, needs to combine a strong desire for living with a strange carelessness about dying. He must not merely cling to life, for then he will be a coward, and will not escape. He must not merely wait for death, for then he will be a suicide, and will not escape. He must seek his life in a spirit of furious indifference to it; he must desire life like water and yet drink death like wine. No philosopher, I fancy, has ever expressed this romantic riddle with adequate lucidity, and I certainly have not done so. But Christianity has done more: it has marked the limits of it in the awful graves of the suicide and the hero, showing the distance between him who dies for the sake of living and him who dies for the sake of dying."

(G.K. Chesterton, Orthodoxy)

Be en-couraged. Be injected with supernatural courage by the grace of God. Your courage is waiting to lay hold of the promises of God, arrest men and rewrite history.

DAY 84
TRUE PEACE

"Do you suppose that I came to bring peace on the earth? I tell you, not at all, but rather division."
Jesus (Luke 12:51)

Peace is not the absence of conflict but the presence of Jesus. True peace is only found when you have peace with Almighty God, through Jesus Christ. This eternal peace is only ever the other side of every other false peace. The cage must be violated before the bird is set free. Or as Richard Rohr writes, *"Before the truth sets you free, it tends to make you miserable."*

Many a false prophet today cries "Peace, peace", even the devil himself, so long as you preach not the cross and His gospel of salvation. Jesus says, *"Blessed are the peacemakers, for they shall be called the children of God"* (Matthew 5:9). As Bernard of Clairvaux writes, *"Consider carefully that it is not the people who call for peace but those who make peace who are commended."*

Peace is neither an intellectual, political notion nor has anything to do with our level of comfort. Peace is a spiritual reality and impartation that has to do with dethroning Satan and enthroning Jesus, Prince of Peace. Peace is made through the gospel alone and why the Apostle Paul, John Wesley and the saints throughout the ages have cried, *"For I am not ashamed of the gospel of Christ, for it is the power of God to salvation for everyone who believes."*

Anxiety is the tireless quest to suck life and peace from the wrong tap. His church are the merchants of the ultimate hope and the only true peace.

DAY 85
THE RICHES OF CONTENTMENT

*"If you are not content with what you have, you
would not be satisfied if it were doubled."*

Charles Spurgeon

God often won't change our circumstances until we relinquish trust in them being the source of our longed-for security, rest, and abundant life. He is too good and loves us too much to allow us to remain victims and addicts, poor in soul, who trust in broken cisterns for life, which can never ultimately satisfy. The wilderness forces the question: is His portion enough?

Paul exhorts: "Rejoice always, pray without ceasing and in everything give thanks." (1 Thessalonians 5:16-18) The rejoicing, prayer and gratitude 'always', 'unceasing' and 'in everything' is the key here. When we carry a righteous heart-posture irrespective of our circumstances, we have begun to mature in the site of heaven and to walk in the abundant life that Jesus promised (John 10:10).

Paul wrote, "I have learned to be content in whatever state I am" (Philippians 4:11). The abundant life of contentment must be learnt, which comes with maturity. I am not living abundantly if I am still a victim of my circumstance. Something or someone other than Jesus has become Lord. God wants us to know that the kingdom of God really is within us and that anything and everything is possible despite what's happening on the outside, circumstantially. As Jesus once modelled, nation changers snooze in storms with happy dreams.

Jesus modelled abundant life and came to give us abundant life. He is not letting us be until we get it, however much we kick and scream! The contentment of abundant life says, "I am able to live fully in the season I am in. I am not going to be anxious.

I am going to thrive and live thankfully." Abundant life is 'living with a full heart". Bill Johnson says, "Living in abundance involves staying in your lane and thriving in the place and season God has you in."

When you can celebrate others' breakthrough and blessing, it says an awful lot about the state of your heart and the Lordship of Jesus (as opposed to something else) in your life. In effect, it qualifies you for your own blessing and demonstrates that you could handle the persecution that it might/will bring. You could handle it being taken from you. The thing doesn't own you, it hasn't become Lord.

Bill Johnson goes on to say, "Living in abundance with contentment does involve having dreams – a bigger house, a spouse and family, a larger company, a more influential ministry. The Father loves to position us for increase. But when my dreams make me anxious, they disturb the Lordship of Jesus." Those who are thankful in their present state are the richest people on earth.

Your patience and levels of gratitude are indications of your surrender, your trust and your freedom. Can you rejoice whatever the situation, can you give thanks whatever storm is blowing? Is your prayer life and intimacy with the Father constant, merely because His glorious presence is your chief portion? That is true contentment. That is abundant life. That is freedom.

DAY 86
FEAR, POVERTY, FAITH AND WEALTH
PART 1

*"When the party is about to die, Jesus turns
water into wine. And it's the best vintage. Jesus
came to demonstrate what God looks like."*
Kris Vallotton

The Apostle Paul wrote this to the Corinthian church:

*"Yes, God is more than ready to overwhelm you with every
form of grace, so that you will have more than enough of
everything —every moment and in every way. He will make
you overflow with abundance in every good thing you do."*

2 Corinthians 9:8 (TPT)

Do you associate Christianity with "overwhelming grace", "more
than enough", "overflow" and "abundance"? Allow me to ask
you another question: When you think of God, do you think of
Him giving the best? I wonder how long Adam and Eve wrestled
with this question, upon meeting the serpent.

For many years, particularly before I knew Jesus, I was
incapacitated by fear of failure. Fear was the driver to most things
in my life, often subconsciously. Despite being relatively wealthy
and successful in the world's eyes, I was poor at the deepest
level because of the place fear had in my life. I feared risk. I often
feared the opinions of man. I dreaded sacrifice and hard work,
partly because hard work had always carried connotations of
boredom to me, rather than satisfaction and excitement. I didn't
live to work with heavenly purpose, I worked to get work out of
the way, so that then I could "live". Little did I know that abundant
life was in Jesus all the while and not in "free time." I worked

as a slave to the things society said I needed to be and to have in order to be acceptable. I was a servant of stuff, reputation, rejection and fear – in truth I was a bound and lost idolater.

Fear lives small. Faith, working through love (for God and man) lives large. This is true wealth. The children of God are called to a wealth mindset. How do you know whether you are living under a poverty or a wealth mindset?

Wealth is the ability to rejoice in another's success, to no longer feel that pinch of "elder brother" envy, the evidence of a poverty spirit from the orphan stable. Wealth is a "more than enough" mindset, and a "nothing is impossible belief" system. True wealth is not necessarily financial riches (financially rich people can be deeply poor on the inside) but it does involve money and financial blessing. Wealth is radical generosity, extraordinary compassion, sacrificial giving and profound humility. True wealth acknowledges grace at every turn – a good Father from whom every good thing comes. Wealth doesn't merely survive, it finds a way to thrive, to build, it never gives up dreaming and it looks to leave a legacy. Wealth is always thankful and never jealous, it does not brag, it celebrates others and it glistens with hope for the future.

DAY 87
FEAR, POVERTY, FAITH AND WEALTH
PART 2

"You will always reflect the nature of
the world you're most aware of."
Bill Johnson

Every person is a mirror to their true altar – we reflect the glory or misery of the god or God we choose to focus upon. As we seek God with all our hearts, surrendered unto His purposes, what has eternal value will begin to burn on our hearts.

In Matthew 25 Jesus tells a parable about talents, stewardship, faith and fear.

> *"For the kingdom of heaven is like a man traveling to a far country, who called his own servants and delivered his goods to them. And to one he gave five talents, to another two, and to another one, to each according to his own ability; and immediately he went on a journey. Then he who had received the five talents went and traded with them, and made another five talents. And likewise he who had received two gained two more also. But he who had received one went and dug in the ground, and hid his lord's money. After a long time the lord of those servants came and settled accounts with them."*

This parable is a picture of the Day of Reckoning. What are we doing with what God has given us? Are we living from fear or faith? Two servants steward what God has given them through faith, one hides in fear. As I have explained, for many years I lived from fear, like an orphan, hiding my full expression. This is how most of the world lives. Jesus said that as you steward faithfully what God has given you, you will even be given the talents that others have hidden. – "So take the talent from him, and give it to him who has ten talents. 'For to everyone who has, more will be given, and he will have abundance; but from him who does not have, even what he has will be taken away.'" (Matthew 25:28-29). These are strong words; stewardship and prosperity of soul (even finances) are big deals to God, despite what many religious types might say.

We need to have an abundance mentality in this hour, not a poverty mindset. Jesus said I came to give life in *"abundance"* (John 10:10). There is no poverty or lack in heaven. The church are not called to be orphans who scrape by but sons and daughters of the King called to manifest heaven on earth. Blessed and influential, according to our call (our "lane") to be a blessing and influencer.

Take you talents and invest them in the kingdom of God. Watch them grow for His purposes and glory. Hard work is a joy when it is fuelled by the grace of God, precious to His heart and unto eternal reward.

> *"Our greatest fear should not be of failure but of succeeding at things in life that don't really matter."*
>
> (D.L. Moody)

LOVE, HATE AND ANGER
PART 1

*"Love must be sincere. Hate what is evil;
cling to what is good."*
Romans 12:9

Bill Johnson said this: 'I feel like there is a gift of anger that God wants to release. There is a passivity that has been exalted as being Christ-like. And things happen around us that are supposed to matter. They are supposed to cause pain and if they don't cause me pain and provoke me to a righteous anger then I am dead. I am dead to what is supposed to be happening inside me. But that anger is not released or aimed at people and that is the challenging part . . . True anger says "this is not happening on my shift." And we give ourselves to pray because there is a power at work that must be shut down.'

What you hate will tell me what you love. What gets you angry will tell me what you crave and long for, whom and what you wish to protect. Jesus flipped tables in anger and disgust because intimacy with God had been sacrificed for greed and commerce. Jesus sternly rebuked the early church because His Bride-to-be had begun to tolerate false teaching, sexual sin, vapid consumerism and lukewarm living (Revelations 2-3). Jesus hates evil. And we must. Because He loves people! Love isn't politically right, it is right with God. God's judgment is always towards whatever interferes with true love.

One measure of our love for Jesus is manifest in the degree to which we hate evil. This notion that Christians just love and tolerate everything is erroneous and a doctrine that has been cooked up by the very devil in hell. We are called to love God, and love people, as we love ourselves. As a result, we hate the sin that offends God and contaminates and destroys His people, including ourselves. Look at the cross! Grace, mercy, justice and wrath – it all meets there in the bloody body of our Saviour. There's a righteous anger in the saints that longs for justice, birthed by the Spirit within us who yearns jealously.

> *"For God in heaven unveils his holy anger breaking forth against every form of sin, both toward ungodliness that lives in hearts and evil actions. For the wickedness of humanity deliberately smothers the truth and keeps people from acknowledging the truth about God."*
>
> Romans 1:18

Beware, some people need a theology of an angry God to justify their anger against sinners. We can be pretty gifted at projecting our dysfunctions. Feasting on "the angry God in the sky" can also justify or act as a vent to our anger at life and its sufferings. In both of the above cases the theology is abused and will carry a dark spiritual impartation, flavoured with condemnation and lacking love and grace. I have known this operate in my own life and the fruit is never good. "The heart is deceitful, who can know it . . . ?"

But let's not throw the baby out with the dirty bath water. When we react to error we always create more error. Theological abuse in the church does not excuse us from stewarding a faithful understanding of the wrath of God and what that means for us. As A.W. Tozer writes:

> *"Whatever is stated clearly but once in the Holy Scriptures may be accepted as sufficiently well established to invite the faith of all believers; and when we discover that the Spirit speaks of the wrath of God about three hundred times in the Bible we may as well make up our minds either to accept the doctrine or reject the Scriptures outright. If we have valid information from some outside source proving that anger*

is unworthy of God, then the Bible is not to be trusted when it attributes anger to God. And if it is wrong three hundred times on one subject, who can trust it on any other? The instructed Christian knows that the wrath of God is a reality, that His anger is as holy as His love, and that between His love and His wrath there is no incompatibility."

DAY 89
LOVE, HATE AND ANGER
PART 2

"Be angry and sin not."
(Ephesians 4:26)

In one degree or another, anger is our response to whatever endangers something we love. "In its uncorrupted origin," says Tim Keller, "anger is actually a form of love" ("The Healing of Anger"). Anger is love in motion to deal with a threat to someone or something we truly care about. God is angry at sin because He loves people. But God is able to love people unconditionally whilst being angry at our sin. God never turns His immeasurable love off and He never turns His righteous anger off. This is what makes Him God, perfect love, and perfect light.

So what does this mean for us? Anger points to our loves, for good or evil. Some anger is an outworking of our lust for control, ultimately pointing to the idol in our life that is being poked and threatened. In contrast, a lack of anger, or indifference at the turmoil and suffering in the world, ought to make us question whether we love anything at all. And a lack of righteous anger in the church usually owes to the oppression of a religious or political spirit, an increased worldliness, a dumbing down of the scriptures and so a dim view for what breaks God's heart.

We must watch our motives. Where is our love really pointed? What is at the root of our hatred and anger and so where is our anger really pointed? Is the root of our anger pride, bitterness, resentment, a critical spirit or is it a love for God, His word, His people and a hatred of sin and injustice? Is the fruit of our anger impatient reaction, strife, ungodly fear or is it deepened intercession, compassion for the broken and pulling down strongholds? Is the fruit of our anger graceless condemnation or firm correction through love unto redemption and restoration? The fruit always reveals the root and that's how we are known in heaven.

When we are angry we must ask the Holy Spirit to search our hearts – for carnal wrath does not produce the righteousness of God. (James 1:19-20) Hot-temperedness is foolish and unrighteous. We must be slow to anger. Be angry and sin not. I like how Tim Keller puts it: in the Kingdom of God love is not no anger, or blow anger (quick to blow up) but slow anger.

Importantly, Saints are not in the hands of an angry god. For those who have come to the cross and accepted Jesus, the wrath of God has been exhausted in His body on the tree and every Christian can approach the Day of Judgement with confidence.

So what gets you righteously angry? It can reveal your calling. A God without wrath is a God without love for His children and a church without righteous anger is a people without compassion, truth, shallow on commission. May the Lamb of God receive His reward through a mature expression of divine love working through His church. Don't let the religious spirit button you up like a pious mouse. Neither let the enemy poke a wound of rejection nor massage your ego to react from the flesh. When tables need to be flipped for Christ's sake, flip them. When the lion of Judah needs to roar against lies, sin and injustice, roar – but do all from that place of compassionate love. Let's learn to walk in sincere love by hating what is evil and clinging to what is good.

DAY 90
LOVE IN THE FACE OF INTIMIDATION

"When you're 20 you care what everyone thinks,
when you're 40 you stop caring what everyone
thinks, when you're 60 you realise no one was
ever thinking about you in the first place. You
have enemies? Good. That means you've stood
up for something, sometime in your life."
Winston Churchill

Perhaps our nation's greatest ever preacher, George Whitefield, said this: *"If you are going to walk with Jesus Christ, you are going to be opposed . . . In our days, to be a true Christian is really to become a scandal."*

Sadly, in today's western climate, you will be called a bigot for speaking the truth in love. It's a given. As in Whitefield's day, our faith has become scandalous and will be opposed. But know this: you have been bullied by a true bigot, in the true sense of the word. Let's look the word up. A bigot is 'a person who is intolerant towards those holding different opinions.' This is the level of hypocrisy and deception many have sunk to today. But deception can be a red carpet for our compassion, because many are simply unaware (by definition deception means you are deceived and so ignorant), they have swallowed sound-bites from the wrong source (this stuff is all over the university campuses) and ours is the role to bring revelation and truth, in love, in order to set free.

"The new brand of political correctness, popular on college campuses and social media, is the idea that no speech should exist that directly challenges politically correct ideas. Liberals label all speech they don't like as "hate speech." That term has been stretched so broadly it has lost all meaning. The

practitioners of the new political correctness are not equipped for a world in which individuals can disagree with what is deemed appropriate thought. They rely on silencing the opposition with hysterics, instead of winning with superior ideas. Freedom of speech is America's most cherished right, and implicit in freedom of speech is the freedom to disagree."

Milo Yiannopoulos

Sadly, I suspect I haven't preached a full gospel if 'bigot' mud isn't somewhere on my coat as I finish up! So be encouraged church, let's learn to celebrate persecution like never before, knowing that if God is for us, who cares who's against us? Remember, this important topic of persecution takes up two verses in the central beatitudes (more than any other), yet I fear we don't dine out here nearly long enough in today's assemblies.

"How enriched you are when you bear the wounds of being persecuted for doing what is right! For that is when you experience the realm of heaven's kingdom. How ecstatic you can be when people insult and persecute you and speak all kinds of cruel lies about you because of your love for me! So leap for joy – since your heavenly reward is great. For you are being rejected the same way the prophets were before you."

(Matt 5:11-12)

Jesus says, persecution is evidence of our prophetic role. If we are not being persecuted on some level, we are not evidencing godliness, the kingdom of God is not advancing through our lives (Acts 14:22). Persecution leads to stunning eternal reward and God uses it to further His cause in the earth. Read the book of Acts, the church spread like wildfire largely through persecution. So rejoice, the Lord God almighty reigns! And let perfect love cast out intimidation.

DAY 91
FROM INTIMIDATION TO AUTHORITY

*"Many believed in His name when they saw
the signs which He did. But Jesus did not
commit Himself to them, because He knew
all men, and had no need that anyone should
testify of man, for He knew what was in man."*

John 2:23-25

What I am about to say is not just theory, I have walked this out, been on both sides of the equation. You cannot have the anointing of the Spirit of God whilst desiring man's respect. Many ministers in the church walk in no power or anointing, their preaching is dry, lifeless and carnal, because they have forfeited their authority and grieved the Holy Spirit, by bowing at the altar of the praise of man. If you repent, God will set you free and you will preach with great power, setting the captives free, including yourself. You will know a whole new level of inspiration, revelation and anointing.

Intimidation and political correctness are great snare in this hour. Intimidation looks to feed from self and pride. Intimidation forces the question: "What is going to happen to me?" It resulted in the mighty, fearless, false-prophet-slaying Elijah capitulating to Jezebel, running for his life and coming under depression and suicide. Selah. Perfect love (loving God, being filled by His love and loving others, denying self) casts out all fear.

If you filter what you are going to say via this enemy of intimidation, which rides on the back of political correctness, you have in reality bowed to the devil and so are held captive. Your life and message will have no power, confusion will abound, and sin will grow amidst your congregation. Never sacrifice the anointing for respectability. Fear God only, preach at His unction and inspiration alone and you will become an unsullied conduit for the word of God to flow powerfully by the Spirit and your congregation will have the victory. Salvation, healing and deliverance will break out.

DAY 92
BOLD ZEALOTS
PART 1

"I know your works, that you are neither cold nor hot. I could wish you were cold or hot. So then, because you are lukewarm, and neither cold nor hot, I will vomit you out of My mouth. Because you say, 'I am rich, have become wealthy, and have need of nothing' – and do not know that you are wretched, miserable, poor, blind, and naked – I counsel you to buy from Me gold refined in the fire, that you may be rich; and white garments, that you may be clothed, that the shame of your nakedness may not be revealed; and anoint your eyes with eye salve, that you may see. As many as I love, I rebuke and chasten. Therefore be zealous and repent."

Jesus (Revelation 3:15-20)

A temptation to which we must all say "no" is the craving to be considered cool by the world, even cool to the church. What we really want is for heaven to see us as hot – zealous for Jesus. Zeal means "great energy or enthusiasm in pursuit of a cause or an objective." Here are some synonyms: passion, ardour, love, fervour, fire, avidity, devotion, enthusiasm, eagerness, keenness, appetite, relish, gusto, vigour, energy, intensity. Holy Spirit zeal is deeply attractive to heaven. But zeal for Jesus will look foolish to the world and it will stink to some in the church. Beware of its opposites: apathy and lukewarmness – these are revolting to Jesus, as we read above, and He's the audience we need to concern ourselves with.

I hear many people say that their faith is "personal", that it's something they "keep to themselves", that they have "a quiet"

Christian faith. Often the above is said in a tone suggesting that this is somehow noble or humble. Many of us have bought into a religious lie. We are strangled by tradition. Yes, our church meetings must have a degree of order and measure. Our witness must be spiritually sensitive. But we need to own the fact that many of us have simply left our First Love, walked away from the Great Commission, lost our passion for the lost, bowed to the fear of man and dignity and called it wisdom. We need to repent and get our spiritual fire back. Jesus commands "Be zealous." (Revelation 3:20)

Jesus also commands us to "preach" His gospel (Mark 16:15). Preaching (Greek word "kerusso") isn't quiet and personal. It's a public announcement in the manner of a herald. There is nothing in the Bible that says there's anything noble about a "quiet" Christian faith! You can't find it in the New Testament expression of church. Read Acts and you'll find Pentecost, persecution and prison, revival, riot and revolution. Our prayer life might be quiet and contemplative but the deep river it births will produce a powerful flow of speech and bold unction to the glory of God. We glorify God with our tongues.

"All you thirsty ones, come to me! Come to me and drink! Believe in me so that rivers of living water will burst out from within you, flowing from your innermost being, just like the Scripture says!"

(John 7:37-38)

DAY 93
BOLD ZEALOTS
PART 2

"A zealous man in religion is pre-eminently a man of one thing. It is not enough to say that he is earnest, hearty, uncompromising, thorough-going, whole-hearted, fervent in spirit. He sees one thing, he cares for one thing, he lives for one thing, he is swallowed-up in one thing – and that one thing is to please God. Whether he lives – or whether he dies; whether he has health – or whether he has sickness; whether he is rich – or whether he is poor; whether he pleases man – or whether he gives offence; whether he is thought wise – or whether he is thought foolish; whether he gets blame – or whether he gets praise; whether he gets honor, or whether he gets shame – for all this the zealous man cares nothing at all. He burns for one thing – and that one thing is to please God, and to advance God's glory. If he is consumed in the very burning – he is content. He feels that, like a lamp, he is made to burn, and if consumed in burning – he has but done the work for which God appointed him. Such a one will always find a sphere for his zeal. If he cannot preach, and work, and give money – he will cry, and sigh, and pray. Yes, if he is only a pauper, on a perpetual bed of sickness – he will make the wheels of sin around him drive heavily, by continually interceding against it. If he cannot fight in the valley with Joshua – then he will do the prayer-work of Moses, Aaron, and Hur, on the hill. (Exodus 17:9-13.) If he is cut off from working himself – he will give the Lord no rest until help is raised up from another quarter, and the work is done. This is what I mean when I speak of "zeal" in religion."

J.C. Ryle

God is zealous. There is a very special place in His heart for zealots. Phinehas is my personal favourite, with Elijah, John the Baptist, the Apostles Peter and Paul in shared second place. Phinehas (Aaron the priest's grandson) threw a javelin at two rebellious Israelites killing them on the spot. God said that Phinehas' "zeal" turned away His wrath and judgement and ended the plague on Israel which had killed 24,000 people. That's pretty intense. The zeal of Phinehas, which God actually describes as 'My zeal', the zeal of the Lord, actually 'made atonement' for Israel (Numbers 25:7-13). Selah.

Of course, in the New Testament, our passion, violence and zeal are not physical but spiritual. This tells us that our God, who changes not, is far less manicured, mild, politically correct and far more fiery, passionate and zealous than most of our quaint religious ways would suggest. In Revelation 3:19, Jesus makes it clear that zeal is a requirement for the believer and that lukewarm living as a Christian is sick-making to Him. Let the Holy Spirit-quenching church throw down her buckets of cold water and the zealots of the church of Jesus Christ come forth. May the Body of Christ burn with zeal and wisdom once again.

DAY 94
MEEKNESS

"You have no questions to ask of any body, no new way that you need inquire after; no oracle that you need to consult; for whilst you shut yourself up in patience, meekness, humility, and resignation to God, you are in the very arms of Christ, your heart is His dwelling-place, and He lives and works in you."

William Law

Meekness is the absence of complaint. The tongue is bridled in the delight of the fear of God.

As control follows fear, so does meekness follow trust. The meek inherit the earth – they own nothing but possess everything.

Fear controls in an attempt to be first. Faith is meek, comfortable with being last. In the end God ensures they swap places.

DAY 95
THE POWER OF PROCLAMATION

"For as the rain comes down, and the snow from heaven,
And do not return there,
But water the earth,
And make it bring forth and bud,
That it may give seed to the sower
And bread to the eater,
So shall My word be that goes forth from My mouth;
It shall not return to Me void,
But it shall accomplish what I please,
And it shall prosper in the thing for which I sent it."

Isaiah 55:10-11

Derek Prince said this:

"Many Christians are not aware of this amazing potential that is available to them. No matter what we are facing, as we learn to proclaim the Word of God, God's creative, transforming power is released."

(The Power of Proclamation)

The word of God is the most powerful force in the universe. Right now, it's holding both you, this book or your LED device together at a sub-cellular level (Hebrews 1:3). The devil wants to do two things to the church: get her to dilute and compromise the word of God, or intimidate her into complete silence. With either result, he wins, the church loses.

"Did God really say this?" "Did God say that?" "You can't say that. And don't you dare say that in public . . ." (Genesis 3, Matthew 4) Church, stop agreeing with all the drivel of the devil in the world. The devil is a liar! We are like Isaiah, amidst a people of unclean lips. We need a live coal of fire from the altar to purge our sin and make us ready for sending.

I am neither interested nor impressed by what modern man is capable of. What gets me excited is the Holy Spirit with a sword in His hand. "Take the sword of the Spirit, which is the word of God." – Ephesians 6:17. If we want to see God wield the violence of His love and redemption, then we must preach His word ceaselessly and faithfully.

Today, bridle your tongue, feast on truth, come into agreement with heaven and proclaim His word. Just as in the beginning, the Holy Spirit is brooding over the chaos and deep darkness, it takes just one word from heaven to bring the Spirit's supernatural life and light. His saints are the prophetic vessels. Preach! Proclaim boldly! Preach with expectation! Now is not the time for silence and not the time for apology.

DAY 96
THE LONGING FOR JUSTICE
PART 1

*"There's nothing hippie about my picture of Christ.
The gospels paint a picture of a very demanding,
sometimes divisive love, but love it is."*

Bono

If God is love, how can there be a hell? That question trips off the tongue easily in our morally relativist, decadent, secular, God-embarrassed times. Hitler killed 11 million people; teenage girls were hung by the neck as partisans whilst Nazi soldiers looked on and laughed. If God is good, not to mention holy and just, how can there not be judgement, punishment and hell? But none of us get off by pointing the finger at the great "wickeds" of history. We're all guilty.

People tell me they are "good people" and deserve heaven. Well, have they never told a lie? Have they never stolen anything? Have they never used and trampled upon another human being to get their selfish needs met? The truth is human beings believe in and want justice far more than they will seemingly "allow" a holy God to execute it.

When people steal our stuff, we expect punishment. Either way, we usually deliver our own punishment, passively or actively. When there is rape and murder, we all crowd around the courtrooms. The newspapers and the pubs cry out for justice every day. We want justice. We crave justice. It's in our nature. We just don't want it to interfere with our bespoke life of selfish, sinful, godless idolatry.

God is absolutely right and just to punish wickedness. We ought to thank God that one Day there will be perfect justice executed. Yet the Bible says that God takes no pleasure in the death of the wicked. He wants us all to repent and come to the knowledge of the truth. Mercy, grace, complete forgiveness and salvation have been made available in Christ Jesus before the great and terrible Day of the Lord.

Jesus was judged in our place. There is the mercy of God. Hell was not created for man. The scripture clearly states that hell was created for the devil and his angels. However, if we refuse the mercy of Jesus at Calvary then for God to remain a just God, we must face His judgment and receive His dreadful punishment (Matthew 25:46). Put another way, if God refused to forgive sin at all then He would be just but He wouldn't be merciful. But if God forgave us without the cross He would be merciful but He wouldn't be just. Both the mercy and justice of God meet at the cross alone. That's why Jesus Christ is the only way to heaven. (John 14:6)

THE LONGING FOR JUSTICE
PART 2

But He was wounded for our transgressions, He was bruised for our guilt and iniquities; the chastisement [needful to obtain] peace and well-being for us was upon Him, and with the stripes [that wounded] Him we are healed and made whole. All we like sheep have gone astray, we have turned everyone to his own way; and the Lord has made to light upon Him the guilt and iniquity of us all."
Isaiah 53:5-6 (AMPC)

Atheism is an excuse to live as we want without responding to our inbuilt conscience. Check this out:

"God's [holy] wrath and indignation are revealed from heaven against all ungodliness and unrighteousness of men, who in their wickedness repress and hinder the truth and make it inoperative. For that which is known about God is evident to them and made plain in their inner consciousness, because God [Himself] has shown it to them.

For ever since the creation of the world His invisible nature and attributes, that is, His eternal power and divinity, have been made intelligible and clearly discernible in and through the things that have been made (His handiworks). So [men] are without excuse [altogether without any defense or justification].

Because when they knew and recognized Him as God, they did not honor and glorify Him as God or give Him thanks. But instead they became futile and godless in their thinking [with vain imaginings, foolish reasoning, and stupid

speculations] and their senseless minds were darkened. Claiming to be wise, they became fools"
(Romans 1)

The knowledge of God is inbuilt in all of us. Creation screams an Intelligent Designer's fingerprints. Our conscience daily speaks of a coming Judgement Day. We are all going to die, meet our Maker and answer to that conscience before Him. Fifty-four million people die every year. The reality of eternity is coming for all of us; not as a whimsical "RIP" puff of well-earned release but a freight train of conscient, cognisant, sensual dread and ecstasy (depending on your Advocate and covering) before a Great White Throne of judgment. Liars are suppressing that truth. Small wonder that St Paul (in the same chapter of Romans) insisted he wasn't ashamed of the gospel but, on the contrary, described himself as a "debtor to all men" to open his mouth and proclaim it with boldness.

Bono said this: "If there's no God, it's serious. If there is a God it's even more serious." May we truth-proclaimers take off our self-imposed muzzles and rise up like roaring lions for such a time as this. For Christ's sake and the love of God! The harvest is ripe.

DAY 98
FORGIVENESS CHECK-UP
PART 1

*"To forgive is to set a prisoner free and
discover that the prisoner was you."*
Lewis B. Smedes (Ethicist and Theologian)

Giving someone the cold shoulder (passive aggressive punishment) has nothing to do with healthy boundaries. Such fear-based behaviour is evidence I hold bitterness and unforgiveness. Until I will that person a blessed life I will never be free. When did you last have a forgiveness check-up? No-one puts it better than RT Kendall. Read the following, slowly –
    What total forgiveness is:

1. Being aware of what someone has done and still forgiving them

Total forgiveness is painful. It hurts when we kiss revenge goodbye. It hurts to think of that person getting away with what they did and nobody knowing. But when I know fully what they did, and accept in my heart that they will be blessed without any consequences for their wrong, I have crossed over into the supernatural. This means I have begun to be a little bit like Jesus.

2. It is a choice to keep no records of wrong

Love 'keeps no record of wrongs' (1 Corinthians. 13:5). Why do we keep records? To use them. To prove what happened. To wave it before someone who doubts what actually happened. Love is a choice. Total forgiveness is a choice. It is not a feeling – at first – but an act of the will. It is the choice to tear up the record of wrong.

3. Refusing to punish

This is the essence of total forgiveness. It is when we give up the natural desire to see them 'get what's coming to them'. By nature, we cannot bear the thought that they have got away with what they have done; it seems so unfair. Therefore, we want vengeance – namely, their just punishment. The fear that they won't get punished is the opposite of perfect love.

4. Not telling what they did

As I said above, there may be a need to tell somebody about your own hurt, and this can be therapeutic. But you should tell maybe only one other person and be sure that person will never repeat it. Telling a person with the purpose of hurting another's reputation or credibility is but wanting to punish them.

5. Being merciful

"Blessed are the merciful, for they will be shown mercy" (Matthew. 5: 7). There is a sense in which the Bible basically says two things about God: (1) that He is merciful, and (2) that He is just. The heart of the gospel is related to these two characteristics of God. The greatest question we can ask when it comes to the gospel of Christ is: how can God be just and merciful at the same time? By merciful, it means that God does not want to punish us; by just, it means He must punish us because we have sinned against Him. So how can He be both simultaneously? Answer: He sent His Son Jesus Christ – the God-man – who died on a cross for us. *"We all, like sheep, have gone astray, each of us has turned to his own way; and the LORD has laid on Him the iniquity of us all"* (Isaiah. 53:6). Because God punished Jesus for what we did, He can now be true to Himself and still be truly merciful to us. That is the heart of the gospel.

DAY 99
FORGIVENESS CHECK-UP
PART 2

*"The ultimate proof of total forgiveness takes place
when we sincerely petition the Father to let those
who have hurt us off the hook – even if they have
hurt not only us, but also those close to us."*

R.T. Kendall ('Total Forgiveness')

6. Graciousness

This is showing grace and mercy at the same time. There is an interesting Greek word *erikes*, that means 'forbearance' or 'tolerance'. In Philippians 4:5, it is translated "gentleness" ("moderation" in the Authorised Version). It comes down to our English word 'graciousness'. It is an exceedingly rare quality. It is a word that cuts right across a legalistic spirit (which comes naturally to many of us). It is a concept that is quite threatening to those of us who don't suffer fools gladly, we who feel that being inflexible for the truth is the ultimate virtue. But graciousness is withholding certain facts you know to be true. It is demonstrated by what you don't say, although what you could say would be true. Self-righteous people find it almost impossible to be gracious; they claim always to be after 'the truth'. Total forgiveness is graciousness that will sometimes mean overlooking the truth, and not letting on that you know anything that could damage a person in any way.

7. It is an inner condition

Total forgiveness must take place in the heart for otherwise it is worthless. 'For out of the overflow of the heart the mouth speaks' (Matthew 12: 34). If we have not truly forgiven, in our hearts, those who have hurt us, then it will come out – sooner or later. But if forgiveness has indeed taken place in the heart, our words will show it. When there is bitterness, it will eventually manifest; when there is love, *"there is nothing in him to make him stumble"* (1 John 2: 10), even in our words.

8. It is the absence of bitterness

Bitterness is an inward condition. It is an excessive desire for vengeance that comes from deep resentment. It heads the list of the things that grieve the Spirit of God (Ephesians. 4:30) But how can I know that there is no bitterness left? I would reply: (1) when there is no desire to get even or punish, (2) when I do or say nothing that would hurt their reputation or future, and (3) when I truly wish them well in all they seek to do.

9. Forgiving God

Although we often do not see it at first – and for some it takes a long time – all our bitterness is traceable to our anger towards God. It may be an unconscious anger – some good people would be horrified at the thought that they have bitterness towards God. But we repress this too; such knowledge is too painful to admit to. The truth is, our bitterness is often aimed at God.

10. Forgiving ourselves

Total forgiveness, then, means forgiving people – totally – and also forgiving God. But it also means forgiving ourselves – totally. (Ibid RT Kendall, 'Total Forgiveness')

DAY 100
ROYAL THINKING
PART 1

"Right believing leads to right living."
Joseph Prince

Life is designed to happen from the inside out. We are a spirit, we have a soul and we live in a body. The scripture says, *"As a man thinks in his hearts so is he."* (Proverbs 23:7) In other words, what we believe about ourselves is whom we shall become and this will dictate the way we live. Every kingdom mindset in your daily walk is a landing strip for victorious living. Every lying mindset is a potential destiny-thief. We can ask God to expose the lies so that we can replace every thought with obedience to truth (Christ). Truth will set us increasingly free. John wrote, *"And this is the victory that has overcome the world – our faith"* (1 John 5:4). Our faith, our right believing brings the victory in every circumstance. If I will change my thinking (the essence of repentance), God will change my life. That's good, hope-fuelling news!

"When I am weak, I am strong"
The world revolves around a graceless celebration of self-sufficiency, independence and perfection. This pervasive attitude can stain Christians and bring much hopelessness and condemnation if we are not careful. The truth is weakness, mess and humility attract the Almighty. Surrendered weakness is strength in God's gracious economy and vulnerability and authentic living is beautiful, cultivating intimacy and connection between people. Let's stop faking it! For God can do much more with our confessed weakness, than our projected strength.

I like how Steve Backlund presents the case:

"The next time you think God can't use you in your present state, remember: Abraham was too old, Isaac was a daydreamer, Jacob was a liar and a manipulator, Joseph was abused and in prison, Moses had a stutter, Gideon was fearful and doubting, Samson was a womaniser, Rahab was a prostitute, Jeremiah and Timothy were too young, David had an affair and was a murderer, Elijah was suicidal, Jonah ran from God, Naomi was a widow, Job went bankrupt, Peter denied Christ three times, The disciples fell asleep while praying, Martha worried about everything, the Samaritan woman at the well was divorced (more than once), Zacchaeus was too small, Paul was too religious, Timothy had an ulcer, and Lazarus was dead!"

"Letting go and letting God"

The only person I can control, on a good day, is myself. I can't change people, I can't control people. Whatever I try to control will end up controlling me. The Lord reigns, so I can let go of the need to control. There is freedom in letting go and letting God. John Wesley said, *"Think and let think."* If God sits in the heaven's and laughs at the enemy's plans, then I can learn to also. There is much joy and freedom in this step of faith. Faith laughs. To laugh, you have to let go of something.

"Love is at home with trust and mystery"

The world demands answers and lusts after control. Much of this is rooted in fear. Jesus says *"Follow me and worry not about tomorrow."* Jesus says that the greatest in the kingdom are the child-like. Children love mystery and adventure . . . because they trust that their parents are looking after them.

DAY 101
ROYAL THINKING
PART 2

*"Fix your attention on God. You'll be
changed from the inside out."*

Romans 12:2 (MSG)

"I am always successful"

The scripture reads, *"I can do all things through Christ, who
strengthens me"* (Philippians 4:13). Paul had learned to be
content in any circumstance. This is biblical success. Steve
Backlund comments, *"Success isn't a place to reach, but a Christ-
like state of being. I can be a success if nobody likes me. I can be
a success if everybody likes me. Joseph was always a success.
He was a successful prisoner, a successful slave, a success with
Potiphar ... Wherever you put him he was blessed! Because his
success was on the inside."*

The task-driven world, particularly the West, is woefully bound
by the idols of achievement and materialism. This culture dies
hard in the church, too.

Notwithstanding the good and God-given desire to labour in
His vineyard and to do great things with God, we must understand
that God is far less interested in "what" we are "doing". He is
far more interested in "how" we are "being" and "why" we are
doing what we are. As always, this perfect Father is after our
hearts and our freedom.

God often won't change our circumstances until they have lost
their ability to define us. In fact, He will sometimes purposefully
thwart, disrupt them in order to put His finger on a stronghold
and poke the idol, so that we can emerge from the incident freer
on the inside. Today you are successful from the inside out, by
loving God and people well and being as faithful as you can with

what God has asked of you. That's good news. That in and of itself will turn the world upside down.

"Sonship is enough"

I am learning to rest in my core identity. If I don't have peace being hidden, doing unglamorous things, I'll never have it in the limelight, doing significant things. If I don't have rest when I am broke, I'll never have it when I have lots of money. If I don't have peace single, I won't have it married. The list goes on. Rest is an inside job. It's about the heart. Peace and joy are in the Holy Spirit alone, from the inside, flowing out. Thomas Merton said, *"You find peace not by rearranging the circumstances of your life, but by realising who you are at the deepest level."*

Only when I am secure in my Father's love and my identity as a son am I safe to lead others. Otherwise my leadership will always be to validate me and serve my sense of insignificance. Like Saul with David, I will trample on, or passively undermine (just as wicked) anyone who threatens my position.

Furthermore, I will resent other leaders, compete with them and jealousy will consume me. I will happily spiritualise my dysfunction to cover my barrenness along the way. The heart is deceitful, who can know it? People give their heart and trust to people where they feel loved, safe and believed in. When you are safe in your "chosen-ness" and your place as the beloved, others will feel safe, loved and believed in around you. That's kingdom leadership.

DAY 102
ROYAL THINKING
PART 3

"Love . . . seeks not its own."

St. Paul

"People owe me nothing"

The scripture says, *"Through many tribulations we must enter the kingdom of God"* (Acts 14:22). Amidst the love, joy, peace and blessing of living in the kingdom of God, the faithful Christian will also discover that hard work, betrayal, loneliness, being overlooked, false accusation, dishonour (the list goes on) make up his portion this side of heaven. Bill Johnson said, *"If you don't run into the devil now and then, maybe you are walking in the same direction."* Jesus warned that we should be deeply concerned if everyone speaks well of us. We need to get used to His fragrance on us causing offence, get good at handling it without turning off our love and rejoice in the eternal reward coming. The question remains, how will you handle the tough times? Will they make you bitter or better?

Love is unselfish. We are saved to be love, not *need* love. We are called to love freely; no man is indebted to us. Furthermore, "Love [God's love in us] . . . takes no account of the evil done to it, pays no attention to a suffered wrong" (1 Corinthians 13:5). Love is owed nothing by man – not man's praise, honour, gratitude, apology nor finances. "Debts" are perpetually cancelled, just as Jesus does ours. We are to live in every way unto God, by God, and towards man in truth and love; all else is reserved for the judgement. Love looks for nothing in return and alters not by another's response, believing the best in everyone and choosing to regard no-one after the flesh, but everyone at the end of their race.

How you see the people in your arena of influence is who they will become around you. Simply put, love lives completely without offense. Because self, the ego, is dead. For Christ to live. In this way alone, can I love you unconditionally, by the grace of God. In this way alone, am I free and not being controlled by the thing (or person) I am trying to control. If you believe someone owes you, that there is an unpaid debt, the resentment in your heart will rob your peace, bind you and even make you sick. Forgiveness, every law of God, is for our good.

Welcome to the love war! Lord, help me to bless the haters, live without enemies but also learn what it means to "Let the dead, bury the dead, you follow Me."

DAY 103
ROYAL THINKING
PART 4

*The Lord said to me . . . "If you're not joyful
now, the chances of you being joyful in the
future are slim. Because your lack of joy is not
a circumstantial issue, but a you-issue."*

Steve Backlund

"I rejoice and give thanks always"

Many of us need our circumstances to line up in order to be joyful. The truth is that it's when we rejoice apart from our circumstances that our circumstances become joyful. For joy is a spiritual reality birthed in the presence of God, through right focus and thanksgiving, not a feeling prey to our material world and circumstances. The kingdom of God is always within (for the born-again believer) and at hand for the rest of the world. "In His presence is fullness of joy." (Psalm 16:11)

Suffering, although painful, can actually lead to deepened joy because *"Blessed are those who mourn"* (Matthew 5:4) and rely fully on being regularly flooded by the glorious presence of the Comforter. Trial will either make us bitter or better. That's why Paul writes, *"Rejoice always, in everything give thanks."* We are not made happy by what we acquire but by what we appreciate.

Rejoicing is a command, for our good. When we are not rejoicing, even in the toughest of times, we are prone to complaining, coveting against our neighbour and God and landing in the pit of self-pity. We are slowly becoming deceived and blind to grace. Please don't mishear me: there is *"a time to weep"* (Ecclesiastes 3:4) and *"It is through many tribulations and hardships that we must enter the kingdom of God"* (Acts 14:22).

Life can be filled with hardship and tragedy but there is always something we can be thankful to God for.

Jesus says this: *"In the world you have tribulation and trials and distress and frustration; but be of good cheer [take courage; be confident, certain, undaunted]! For I have overcome the world"* (John 16:33). Our faith, our cheer, lays hold of the overcoming grace of Jesus. In order to lay hold of one thing you often have to let go of another. In order to be joyful, to laugh, you have to let go of something else. Remember grace, remember Calvary, remember Emmanuel, God with us and for us.

The humble and faith-fuelled posture of thanksgiving actually attracts grace, multiplication and increases joy. What you focus on gets larger. As you focus on your blessings, what you do have, the things you lack, in some instances think you lack, will slowly disappear in your renewed vision of abundance. The most thankful people are the most joyful. Not everything will ever be perfect so learn to focus on the good, be thankful, let something go and rejoice!

DAY 104
ROYAL THINKING
PART 5

"There is not one blade of grass, there is no color in this world that is not intended to make us rejoice."

John Calvin

"Thankfulness is true riches!"

I like to think of rejoicing as the zealous, excited proclamation of thanksgiving. I like what my friend Mike Maeshiro writes:

"Many people see what's wrong with their life, what prayer hasn't been answered, what difficulty or struggle still persists, what's missing and how they're not taken care of. This manifests in the form of complaining. It's a cancer of the soul and the epitome of poverty. Am I saying we should deny our experience or ignore our needs? Of course not. But what we focus on increases. And what we observe stimulates more of that observance so we can see it more clearly and more often.

This poverty invites comparison and competition. It turns our neighbour's success into a threat, their victory into a taunt. We cannot celebrate when we are offended, we cannot agree when we are opposed. In our brokenness of thought, we fail to recognise the beauty of what is all around us. When we become calloused to our own blessings, we welcome the devourer to consume more of them.

Every day, constantly, there is an energy available to us to charge our lives with purpose and fulfilment. This energy is a conductor. Through it, we are opened to receive beauty in this life. When we give in to the nature of this energy, it takes anything around us and turns it into a portal through which we are transported to the real us. We can touch the divine and enjoy infinity in a moment, limitless possibility, the assurance of our provision, the fulfilment of our desires; we touch God. This energy manifests in the form of gratitude.

Every single one of us has the means to let the vitality that comes from gratitude flow through us. Waking up in the morning, the house we live in, the fact that we can read this . . . the air in our lungs. We are not lacking in materials to stoke the fires of thankfulness. It's not enough to refrain from complaining. We must cherish the goodness in our lives. When we stop expressing the humility of appreciation and thankfulness, we stop our hearts from recognising gratitude altogether. When we honour gratefulness within us, it allows us to experience more gratitude."

DAY 105
ROYAL THINKING
PART 6

*"The invisible kingdom inside a person
ultimately becomes the visible kingdom
around them. We influence the world
around us with what we believe."*

Kris Vallotton

"His presence is my deepest desire"

You have an inconsolable longing in your heart. Part of you is suffocating. Don't numb the loneliness with entertainment, busyness or superficial connection. You were born for the depths, for a different air. Rebel unto salvation. Shut the door. Turn it off. Be still. Let the violent waterfalls and dormant romance within you lay hold of the kingdom of God. That restless longing has been put there reasonably. It is the evidence, the siren for your ecstatic pilgrimage.

Today, one thing is needed. To waste time with the One who holds time and holds your heart. When the inner ache of wilderness robs your capacity to understand, seek the One who gives peace and joy beyond your need to understand. C.S. Lewis said, *"I know now, Lord, why you utter no answer. You are yourself the answer. Before your face questions die away. What other answer would suffice?"*

Hordes around you will peck, scratch, squawk and flap in the dust like chickens but those who wait will soar with the wind of the Spirit like eagles. How blessed you are and how blissful it is to know your poverty. Clear your diary for God's sake!

DAY 106
ROYAL THINKING
PART 7

"The mind is either at war with God or it is being renewed. There is no middle ground."

Bill Johnson

"I rejoice when others are blessed"

"Jonathan spoke well of David to his Father..." (1 Samuel 19:4). When we understand the generous and gracious heart of God, we will manifest it in our own lives to others. I don't compete, compare or criticise; I simply follow Jesus and champion others. We cannot afford to have thoughts in our hearts and words on our lips about people that are not on God's.

Criticism of others is a manifestation of pride and an open door to the poverty spirit. Pride brings what any rational human being should fear most: God's resistance. Our criticisms will bring us to poverty. My Father has a specific purpose and place for me. Man cannot thwart the purposes of God in any man's life. He will bring it to pass. It's all by grace for all us, none of us have anything to boast in. When I can celebrate other's victories I am ready for my own.

"I live to obey not to succeed"

C.S. Lewis writes, *"It is not your business to succeed, but to do right. When you have done so the rest lies with God."* 'Therefore, judge nothing before the time, until the Lord comes, who will both bring to light the hidden things of darkness and reveal the counsels of the hearts. Then each one's praise will come from God.' (1 Corinthians 4:5)

Father, keep me faithful today. I don't need to succeed in the world's eyes; I'll wait. Amen.

DAY 107
STORM SLEEPERS

'But He was in the stern, asleep on a pillow.'
Mark 4:38

Often you feel like a victim in the storm. But increasingly it is the storms of life that that are becoming a victim of your inner reality. Indeed, all the trials and storms around you are each helping to deepen your roots, thicken the walls of your integrity and build immovable character. So dare to rejoice in the trial (James 1:2-4). For every assault is working together for good in your life, as you love Him with a ruthless trust again and again and again. Christ is being formed in you in deeper and more powerful measure (Romans 8:28-29). You are learning to sleep in the storm and so speak to the storm. You are becoming a force against the enemy and for the advance of the kingdom of God that the devil will wish he never went near.

DAY 108
SIT

*"There is no need to exert yourself.
Repose in Him. Count upon His life."*
Watchman Nee

Sit. Rest. "It is finished." At the cross of Christ, the enemy has been defeated. The born-again believer never fights for victory but from victory. Start by being still and basking in the intimate, ecstatic, "yada" knowledge of Almighty God (Psalm 46:10). The individual Christian life begins with a man "in Christ", when by faith we see ourselves seated together with Him in the heavens (Ephesians 2:6). For Christianity begins not with a big DO, but with a big DONE.

The Christian life from start to finish is based upon this principle of utter dependence upon the Lord Jesus. "Sitting" is an attitude of rest. We only advance in the Christian life as we learn first of all to sit down. To sit down is simply to rest our whole weight – our load, ourselves, our future, everything – upon the Lord. We let him bear the responsibility and cease to carry it ourselves. This is the posture of trust – "seated-ness", meekness, carnal strength and orphan-hearted striving, restrained.

The Christian's secret is his rest in Christ. All who sit can walk, run, even strive. Mark the words of Paul – "To this *end* I also labor, striving according to His working which works in me mightily." (Colossians 1:29) We sit forever with Christ that we may walk continuously before men. Christ strives through us. Forsake for a moment our place of rest in Him. Immediately we are tripped up. Our testimony in the world is marred. But abide in Christ. Our position there ensures the power to walk worthy of Him here. (John 15:1-5)

When you are caught in a storm, are you quick to panic and flail for your lives like the disciples (Mark 4:38)? Or can you rest your head on a pillow like Jesus? We only have authority over the storm we can rest in. The secret, first, is not in walking but in sitting; not in doing but in resting in something done. This good Father is waiting until you cease to do ... When you cease doing, then God will begin.

DAY 109
SPIRITUAL FATHERS

"It is easier to prophesy judgment than reformation when our confidence is in the power of sin and its effects instead of the power of the Gospel."

Bill Johnson

Romans 4:17 takes a similar line and it breaks me open –

'"I have made you the father of many nations." He is our example and father, for in God's presence he believed that God can raise the dead and call into being things that don't even exist yet.'

Do we believe that God can raise the dead? Do we call things as they are or do we call things that be not *as though* they are? There is a vast difference. There's a healthy and needed place for correction and rebuke amidst error (2 Tim 3:16). But the prophetic in the church is not to point out dead bones but to speak breath, life and sinew to any dead bones so that the army that God is forming comes to life in the valley!

What and who are we Fathering with our words?

Do we live out of unbelief (faith in what the enemy is up to), working through fear, or faith in the gospel working through love? What are we impressed by? Where is our confidence? What I am impressed by will be what I focus on, what I focus on will grow larger and fill my heart and what fills my heart will fill my mouth and I will call out.

I can't afford to think differently about my life, your life, or our nation's life than God does. Whether it's a Scripture promise that God has highlighted or a prophetic word, I must review them until what is said is what I think. Promises are like the rudder of a ship. Rudders determine the direction of that ship. And what I do with God's promises determines the direction of my thought-life and eventually affects my reality.

It is essential to understand what God thinks of me, others and situations in order to release heaven's destiny. Regardless of circumstances, God's word is true. "Let God be found true, though every man be found a liar" (Rom. 3: 4). Again, we cannot afford to think differently about ourselves or any situation than God does. Jesus didn't live in reaction to the devil but in response to the Father. That is the true prophetic.

I like how Kris Vallotton puts it — "We have the unique role of prophesying not as things are, but as they should be. My prayer for you today is that you would see things from heaven's perspective and release the love of God onto those around you!"

DAY 110
MIND MADE UP

"Love the Lord your God . . .
with every thought that is within you"
Jesus (Matthew 22:37 TPT)

Have you ever been in a rush to get on the train? Then having arrived at the right platform simply jumped on the waiting train only to find that as it pulls away from the station you boarded the wrong train? Then follows the grim, dawning revelation that you are going completely the wrong way and there's little you can do about it before the next stop, with precious time and money wasted.

It's the same with our train of thought. Be under no illusion: your thoughts take you places, literally. Are you choosing the train wisely?

If I do not make up my mind ahead of time that I am going to refuse to board the wrong train of thought, then I will end up at a place in my head where I do not want be, nor ever needed to be. Christine Caine said this: "One of the most important lessons I have discovered is that nothing is as powerful as a mind made up. A mind made up ahead of time has the power to control the way your day goes, the way your life goes. You have the power to control who you become, because you are literally what you think – whether you choose to learn how to consciously control that or not." Proverbs 23:7 says, 'For as a man thinks in his heart so is he'. (AMP)

Repentance means to change our thinking and the direction of our lives back to God, allowing truth to set us free with divine destiny realised (John 8:30-32, Romans 12:2). How beautiful . . . and how crucial then for us to manage our minds? If we don't our minds will manage us. We're in a fight. Note the language

Paul uses: "For although we live in the natural realm, we don't wage a military campaign employing human weapons... We can demolish every deceptive fantasy that opposes God and break through every arrogant attitude that is raised up in defiance of the true knowledge of God. We capture, like prisoners of war, every thought and insist that it bow in obedience to the Anointed One." (2 Corinthians 10:3-5 TPT) Take your thoughts prisoner or they will take you prisoner. And for that we need a sharp sword (Ephesians 6:17).

Paul continues elsewhere, "Stop imitating the ideals and opinions of the culture around you . . . be transformed by the renewing of your mind, that you may prove what is that good and acceptable and perfect will of God." (Romans 12:2, TPT, NKJV) A sanctified thought life is a kiss to God and a kiss from God.

This has been an ongoing fight for me in my journey from shame-filled to shame-free living, and it will likely be for you as well. For example, negative thoughts about myself are not humble, they are proud - I'm arguing with God. If we disregard the destination board and jump on any train, we'll go anywhere. But if we carefully, even violently, choose the train we really want to be on, repenting of ungodly mindsets, we'll only go where God wants to take us – and that's what we want to learn to do.

DAY 111
HOPE

Four words to help you monitor your hope levels:

1. *"Any area without hope in your life is under the influence of a lie."* (Bill Johnson)

2. *"When your memories are greater than your dreams you are already dying! The goal is to honour the past, live in the present, and look to the future. When you live in the past you become like Lot's wife, and if look back long enough you will become a monument instead of a movement."* (Kris Vallotton)

3. *"One can never consent to creep when one feels an impulse to soar."* (Helen Keller)

4. *"Now may the God of hope fill you with all joy and peace in believing, that you may abound (bubble over) in hope by the power of the Holy Spirit."* (Romans 15:13)

Let believing truth (God's word) smash all hopelessness today, make you glisten with hope and spill it on others. Remember, the increase of His government will know no end. That makes Christians prisoners of "hope" – the confident expectation of good things coming.

DAY 112
LOVE

"Where Love is, God is."

Henry Drummond

I could write a spiritual best-seller, but if it isn't birthed in love, the pages are fit for the bonfire. I could fund clean water for the continent of Africa but if love isn't my motivation, the news would go unheard in heaven. I could raise the dead with my tremendous faith, fill stadiums with repenting lost souls but if the fuel isn't love, I am pitifully lifeless. I could have more wisdom, discernment, understanding and insight than Soloman and Saint Paul put together but if love is absent I am nothing. Any amount of knowledge, giving, healing or prophecy this side of heaven is incomplete. In any debate or cause, I might be right, but without love I am eternally wrong.

Love never fails. Love is spacious and long-suffering. Love is persistently kind and gentle. Love is humble and meek, leaving room for God first and then preferring my neighbour in front. Love is absent of self and perfect love, absent of fear. Love is happy hidden, happy last. Empty of ego, love loses one's own life, always finding true life and purpose in the process. Love will end you up in first place.

Love is Holy-Spirit responsive, never reactionary and defensive. Love is crucified and weighty with resurrection life. Love is holy, pure, uncorrupted, married to truth and every word birthed in true love carries grace to build. Love ends up encouraging, always.

Rooted deep in true identity, love never boasts or postures – those empty and tiring habits and tapes have long been forgotten and discarded. Love serves and gives with gracious boundaries. Love keeps no accounts, love has no competition and love celebrates another's victory without the bitter root of jealousy and envy. Love puts the stone down and will take the stones. Love overflows in mercy and fights for justice.

Love trusts and lets go, living from rest and peace. There is no control in love. Joy is the overflow of this cultivated communion and Presence. The joy of love is violence to darkness – true supernatural strength.

Love is the greatest spiritual warfare, the greatest wealth and riches available and the greatest expression of man. Only lovers are free. Whoever walks in love, walks holding hands with God. O God, I'm sorry, help me love. Yes, I am learning to love.

DAY 113
OBEDIENCE

"Obedience is God's love language."
Heidi Baker

Obedience is rooted in the worshipful romance of abandonment and trust. Our trust is the most precious thing we can give anyone. On the flip side, religious striving, restlessness and independence comes out of a shallow understanding of the cross. We must justify our lives through works.

The gospel of grace says, *"It is finished".* The deeper our revelation of the cross, the Father's love and what Jesus has done *for* us, the more our worship will flow through intimacy, trust and then obedience rather than any subconscious unworthiness (pride) in us that craves to bring a sacrificial offering of appeasement on our terms and apart from the grace of God.

I am not to do things *for* God, but to embrace what He is doing *for* me, in me and through me. I can raise the dead, feed the poor, free the sex slave and win millions to Christ without worshipping God. God desires the intimacy of obedience, not sacrifice. Jesus said: *"If you love Me, keep my commands."* Step into maturity in your walk – rest in the rhythm of grace-fuelled, first-love obedience.

DAY 114
THE WORLD'S PROGRESS OR
HEAVEN'S HOLINESS?
PART 1

*"If I profess with the loudest voice and clearest
exposition every portion of the truth of God
except precisely that little point which the world
and the devil are at the moment attacking, I am
not confessing Christ, however boldly I may be
professing Christ. Where the battle rages, there
the loyalty of the soldier is proved. And to be
steady on all the battle fields besides is merely
flight and disgrace if he flinches at that point."*

Martin Luther

I believe that one of the great battles in the hearts of God's people right now is between the call to holiness, or "progressivism", a word that is hugely in vogue in the world right now. As with all deception, the serpent comes with great cunning, the counterfeit is highly palatable and not easy to spot. Allow me to unpack this a little.

God says, "Be holy, for I am holy." But what does that mean? To be holy means to come out from the world, to be filled with the Holy Spirit, set apart unto God and to be sanctified by the truth of God's word (John 17:17). The truth sets us free! God is holy and we are made in His image. Holiness is our home of true happiness, unquenchable freedom, abundant life and unsurpassing joy. In the redemptive grace of Jesus Christ, holiness is the church's true inheritance, holiness is that which our truest self desires most.

Counterfeit 'holiness' is rife and zealous in both the world and church today and, notwithstanding some good intention and important social reform, uses seductive words like "progressive" and "tolerance" to lure its prey into works of self-righteousness and deception apart from the word of God. This is as opposed to Christ-righteousness and obedience to truth, working through love.

The devil is the great deceiver. Perhaps his greatest tool is to twist words, particularly God's (Genesis 3, Matthew 4). The one who comes disguised as an angel of light "hijacks people's moral compass in order to condemn that which is righteous and celebrate what is shameful" (ibid. Joshua Jones, *"Elijah Men Eat Meat"*). We are all looking to grow and make progress in life. This is a noble aspiration! Indeed, in Christ we are called from one level of glory to another, supernatural "progress" that will continue into eternity by the grace of God. As followers of Jesus, we are also called to love all people even as we love ourselves, which will involve vast measures of "tolerance" for all, perhaps better words, love, patience and forbearance. Biblical love goes way deeper than tolerance.

Much of what the world calls "tolerance" today is actually license and indifference — license to sin mixed with an indifference to ultimate consequence. The church of Jesus is called to hate sin and never to "tolerate" it. Why? Because sin destroys and brings death to those we love. What you tolerate, dominates. (Genesis 4:7). Love says you are going to hell over my dead body (John 15:13). There's nothing tolerant about the cross. So, we can see that 'progressivism' sounds noble, loving and "tolerant" but, in reality, it has become a movement that tolerates, even champions sin and unrighteousness in the name of love. This is counterfeit love, unsanctified mercy — a mercy which God is not offering. It is a movement fuelled by the spirit of the world and is leading many into gross bondage, addiction and darkness (John 8:34). Progressivism is rooted in the fear of man, conformed to the patterns of the world and focussed on the shifting sands of temporal values. Whereas a life of holiness is rooted in the fear of the Lord, conformed to the unchanging word of God and set apart unto eternity. Progressivism leads people into bondage and hell, holiness leads people to everlasting freedom starting on this earth and into heaven.

DAY 115
THE WORLD'S PROGRESS OR HEAVEN'S HOLINESS?

PART 2

*"The greatest danger to the Christian church today
is that of pitching its message too low."*

Dallas Willard

Progressivism is in the world and has crept into parts of the church. Relevance has become a counterfeit holiness. Increasingly fearful of our reputation, unbelieving of scripture and spiritually proud of our church growth techniques, many of us have made relevance an idol. Today, we have world-famous church leaders unable to publicly call out basic biblical sin whilst multiple millions around the world watch on and conclude a vain Calvary.

David Sladden writes that there is, however, *"a relevance that Jesus demonstrated – getting out there, knowing where people are at, feeling their pain, talking their language, and meeting their needs – the very opposite of religion, of course. And this has to be on the unnegotiable basis of biblical truth. Part of what cripples much of the church is its sheer irrelevance. Part is departure from biblical truth."*

May we become *truly* relevant via holiness – set apart unto God first and then sent into the marketplace next, and thus able to deliver a lost people out of darkness and into His glorious light. A holiness that is (always) "non-religious", practical and born into the dirty mangers of our broken world. Jesus was so holy that religious leaders called him a glutton, drunkard and friend of sinners (Luke 7:34). Try camping out there for a while. Holiness means that we are set apart to God first and then sent into the thick of it as a friend. Full of grace, full of truth.

The *falsely* relevant church sacrifices the absolute truths of God, and with those the anointing of the Spirit, on the altar of human reasoning and the praise and acceptance of man. The church without mixture will move in the Spirit without measure. Holy, set apart, and sent in.

DAY 116
GRACE AND REPENTANCE

*"Repentance, not proper behaviour or even
holiness, is the doorway to grace. And the
opposite of sin is grace, not virtue."*

Philip Yancey

We read in the beginning of Mark's gospel that "John came baptizing in the wilderness and preaching a baptism of *repentance* for the remission of sins." (Mark 1:4) In the same chapter it follows – "Now after John was put in prison, Jesus came to Galilee, preaching the gospel of the kingdom of God, and saying, "The time is fulfilled, and the kingdom of God is at hand. *Repent*, and believe in the gospel." (vs 14-15) Finally, the church began her ministry with Peter crying "*Repent*, and let every one of you be baptized in the name of Jesus Christ for the remission of sins; and you shall receive the gift of the Holy Spirit. (Acts 2:38)

Can you spot a pattern here? Repentance alone is the doorway to the grace of the Holy Spirit.

One of the reasons the message of repentance (in this case to the lost) is so key is that in order to receive a Saviour we must know and readily admit that we are a sinner. People who aren't sinners don't need a Saviour. The message of grace is rendered frivolous at best, dangerous and powerless at worst, without apprehending the guilt, consequences and penalty of sin. Don't preach grace apart from law and don't preach law without grace. The cross must be central, not cheap. We must activate our proclamation of the gospel of Jesus with the command to repent unto the gracious, merciful, righteous judge of all because of what Jesus has done. (Mark 1:15, Acts 17:30)

It is the kindness of God that leads to repentance and amidst a stiff-necked people it is the kindness of the messenger to preach repentance. God's kindness is in the cross of His Son Jesus, man's kindness, the daily picking up of his own. Either way, hearts must turn, for without repentance there will be no salvation.

There's a very dangerous false gospel being proclaimed in the church and world today that sidesteps the issue of "sin" (perhaps through embarrassment, the fear of man and being politically correct), often struggling to even mention the word, and has eradicated God's command to repent. Why is the word "sin" important? Well, everyone has an opinion on what is right and wrong, perhaps today more than ever. But sin is God's definition of evil and "righteousness", His definition of good.

The scripture says, *"All unrighteousness is sin"* (1 John 5:17). In other words, there is no grey area with God, whatever is not righteous (what God calls right) is sin. You might not like it that way. But that's the way it is. We must by all means help people to understand the word sin, by explaining it to a biblically illiterate generation, but never redefine what it looks like, nor soften its wages. Stand on the word of God. (2 Tim 3:16)

Never cheapen Calvary by placating what killed the Prince of Life. Let's hit law and death hard and grace, life and resurrection power even harder! The gospel of Jesus reveals both the death sentence of law, sin and judgment and the saving message of grace, mercy and eternal life in Jesus' cross and resurrection – with repentance and faith as our only means of access. This is true love – a church who lays down her life for her friend, one who is not ashamed of the gospel of Jesus Christ, the power of God to save sinners and birth saints.

DAY 117
REBUKE, REPENTANCE AND REST

"Let us hear the conclusion of the whole matter:
Fear God and keep His commandments."
Solomon (Ecclesiastes 12:13)

For each one of us, eternity is only one heartbeat away. The beginning of wisdom is to live in reverential fear of the One to whom we shall soon give account. The end of wisdom to allow that posture to become saturated in faith, working through love – to live as though every day could be our last. It's what Jesus might call Bridal watchfulness (Matthew 25:1-13). Jesus was never reluctant to rebuke and wake people up to the ultimate Day coming for us all, particularly if God's power had been on display.

> *"Then He began to rebuke the cities in which most of His mighty works had been done, because they did not repent: "Woe to you, Chorazin! Woe to you, Bethsaida! For if the mighty works which were done in you had been done in Tyre and Sidon, they would have repented long ago in sackcloth and ashes. But I say to you, it will be more tolerable for Tyre and Sidon in the day of judgment than for you. And you, Capernaum, who are exalted to heaven, will be brought down to Hades; for if the mighty works which were done in you had been done in Sodom, it would have remained until this day. But I say to you that it shall be more tolerable for the land of Sodom in the day of judgment than for you."*
> Jesus (Matthew 11:20-24)

Mighty works, indeed all things which speak of God's grace are to lead to one thing – repentance toward Him. Repentance unto right positioning for Judgment Day. Are you going to Hades or are you born again and fit for heaven? There is no more important question for either you or your loved ones today.

This is what the Sovereign Lord, the Holy One of Israel, says:

"In repentance and rest is your salvation,
in quietness and trust is your strength,
but you would have none of it."

(Isaiah 30:15)

In Matthew 11 Jesus says that the kingdom of God suffers violence and the violent take it by force. In the same chapter Jesus speaks of the rest that only His yoke and the meek, yielded removal of every other yoke, brings. People think rest is a holiday by the beach and a fruit smoothie.

Do you want to know what rest is? It's when you have had all the traffic, the division and the dichotomy of your life removed and you are being found with singleness of heart, singleness of vision, singleness of yoke, no longer living a double life. You have become a single focussed person, found in agreement with Jesus instead of in opposition with Jesus. Do you know what causes traffic? When you worship and pray for hours and then the next day you yield to worldly movies and enter into godless conversations and godless activities. That's what creates traffic in your soul.

Do you want to know how to get into rest – spiritual violence that repents entirely unto unfettered communion. The only way to spiritual rest is spiritual violence. Violence leads to rest. May we once again tremble before God and so rest deep in our souls, calling a whole generation to repentance and salvation. Amen.

'When I heard, my body trembled;
My lips quivered at the voice;

Rottenness entered my bones;
And I trembled in myself,
That I might rest in the day of trouble.'

(Habakkuk 3:16)

DAY 118
PRAISE

"Ever be filled and stimulated with the Holy Spirit."
Ephesians 5:18

Today billions of humans will wander around the earth praising. The only difference will be the object of their praise, their gods or God, and the depth and expression of their praise. Interestingly, the Hebrew root word for praise is "Halal". Our word "hallelujah" comes from this base word. It means "to be clear, to shine, to boast, show, to rave, celebrate, to be clamorously foolish."

For those of us who have been saved from death by the resurrected Jesus Christ and are constantly and freely filled with His glorious Holy Spirit, I wonder what our halal will look like this week and how many lives it will eternally transform? Burn, boast, celebrate and rave, church! We have good reason - the only worthy reason. For God knows this broken earth needs unbridled praise and knowledge of the only true and living God.

You say – "Well, Dom, you don't know what I'm going through!"

I do not. But the activity and conscious energy of praise defiantly acknowledges higher truth. Praising God in difficult times is circumstantial rebellion and aggressive faith in the nature, power and goodness of a God who is above any circumstance, desires to work and save in every circumstance and is worthy of the attention that circumstance so easily steals and lies through. Praise is distilled, uncompromising worship, mainlining adoration to the throne of Almighty God. The praise goes before the breakthrough, the healing, the deliverance, the nation shaking salvation.

DAY 119
INSIDE OUT

"Great leaders emerge from having great
perspectives, not great circumstances."

Jared Neusch

God looks at our hearts, not at the level of polish on the outside of our cup. The world deals in job titles, status and superficial accolade. God desires integrity, character, truth on the inside – to set us free. Who are you when no-one is looking? God looks at "why" we are doing something, not "what" we are doing. The will of God for our lives is more embedded in our "becoming" than our career or doing. It doesn't mean that God doesn't have important assignments for us, or that our occupation or jobs aren't either instrumental or dear to God's heart. But how are you "being"? How are you coping with process?

Let's take a look at what the Bible says about walking like Jesus. First and foremost, are you loving God with everything in you? Are you learning to love yourself by letting God love you, so that you can love others well? When our love for God is all consuming, everything else finds its rightful place. If we seek God and His righteousness first, we can trust that everything needed will follow. (Matthew 6:33)

There is no sacred or secular divide in the kingdom of God. God is unimpressed by whether we're decked out in fine linen, a Savile Row suit, bin liners or purple vestments. Truly there is no partiality with God. You can be an apostle or a waitress, a professor or a student, a CEO or unemployed and flow in the fullness of God's will for your life. But have you taken up your cross, dying daily to self and ego, so that Christ can live?

It matters little if I am a Bishop or a banker, a mother or a lawyer if I am not letting Christ live through me in my heart motivations, in my believing, in the "how" of my life. There is much freedom receiving this freedom from the law, "outward circumcision" in all its guises. All that is needed is *"faith (conviction) activated and energised and expressed and working through love."* (Galatians 5:6)

Let's fall more in love with God. Let's learn to embrace and enjoy the journey, lean into God's process and His being through us, rather than the mirage of arrival – what some have called destination disease. Find out what God is doing and join in. Do great things not for God but with God, remembering the how, the why, the heart behind our actions. Be free in knowing that your circumstances don't define your righteousness. Process, whom we are becoming, is a big deal to God. Ask yourself the question, "Am I becoming love?" We cannot enter into our personal destinies in God unless we allow ourselves to be changed into His likeness. God is after our likeness, our very being, the light, the fragrance and the incense that the sacrificial offering of our lives is releasing wherever we tread.

DAY 120
OUR PART TO PLAY

"The gospel is only good news
if it gets there in time."
Carl F.H. Henry

The cross and resurrection tell me this: "It is finished." Heaven on earth is now available. But how will I respond? My job is to lay hands on the sick. God's job is to heal them. My job is to preach the gospel. God's job is to convict and save. My job is to walk into the unrighteousness marketplace with business, innovation and a culture of honour. God's job is to pour out favour and influence. God has a part. We have a part. God will not do our part. We can't do His part.

Biblical faith is my hungry, compassion-fuelled response to what God has already provided by grace. It's time for the church to repent of all lethargy and fatalism, get spiritually possessive, filled to the brim with the love of Christ and lay hold of that which Jesus has already paid for. His grace, our faith. GO!

DAY 121
LIVE LARGE

*"Put fire in your sermons, or put
your sermons in the fire."*

John Wesley

Just because parts of the church are ashamed of some of the fire in His people . . . Know this: God is a zealous, jealous, consuming fire. He's not ashamed of you. He loves fiery faith. In fact, lukewarm compromise makes Him vomit.

Be free to go big, Saints, to be embarrassing to people, to get your voice back. Get your gospel roar on. We're not called to creep around like kittens. The Father is cheering you on. He wants our love, devotion and fire to spill out everywhere, crashing through all the "safe spaces" and politically neurotic border controls!

You will offend people, that's okay, mainly religious people or overly seeker sensitive, people-pleaser church types. Most of the time we're offended before we're set free. So, don't worry. Jesus offended people, John the Baptist got decapitated for speaking out of turn, St Paul wrote most of the New Testament from prison because he caused civil unrest wherever he preached. Simply please God, follow His lead, shake the dust off your feet, forgive your persecutors, keep your heart soft, your forehead flinty and get on with it. Love lives really large.

SALVATION PRAYER

If you would like to receive all that Jesus has done for you and make Him your Lord and Saviour, please pray this prayer:

Dear Lord Jesus,

I admit that I am a sinner. I have done many things that don't please you. I have lived my life for myself only. I am sorry, and I repent. I ask you to forgive me. Thank you for dying on the cross for my sin. Come into my life. I receive You as my Lord and Savior. Now, help me to live for you the rest of this life.

In the name of Jesus, I pray.

Amen.

Please get connected with a bible-believing, Spirit-filled church and be baptized. If you have any questions contact info@ jesusfields.com

OTHER TITLES BY THE AUTHOR

ISBN 978-1-9083936-4-7

God Hunger is a series of 60 mediations designed to awaken a passion for God's presence. It is an invitation to allow yourself to be transformed into a more passionate, radical follower of Jesus, by His grace.

"Dominic's writing shines with the brilliance that comes from the partnership of hunger and humility. He has a unique ability to make every word count. There is no fluff here – just one powerful sentence after another, filled with kingdom truth. He has woven the Word of God, poignant quotes, and his personal discoveries found in his quest for more of God into a daily reminder of who God says we are. I encourage you to passionately read God Hunger and watch as God satisfies the cry of your heart."

Bill Johnson,
Bethel Church, Redding.